The 7-Steps From Money Slave to Money Master

The Young Adult's Guide to Personal Finance 101: A Quick Start Guide for Teens and College Students

Learn2Thrive Press

Table of Contents

Chapter 1:

Have a Plan and a Blueprint

Without leaps of imagination or dreaming, we lose the excitement of possibilities. Dreaming, after all, is a form of planning. –Gloria Steinem

Money master. The phrase itself sounds too good to be true, right? How can someone master something that everyone is after? What does being a money master entail? In case you are wondering about the validity of your thoughts, don't worry! These questions are perfectly valid.

Becoming a money master or staying in complete control of your finances can seem like a daunting concept. Money can create and solve a lot of problems, so if you can successfully master the skill of controlling it, it could make your life a lot easier. I know it sounds a bit hard to believe, but becoming a money master is actually very achievable if you have the appropriate mindset and the right set of tools. The whole process starts with planning and building a blueprint.

That is why it's always best to start by evaluating the very basic aspects of becoming a money master. Start with understanding your mindset about money and slowly work toward modifying and improving it so you can successfully get started on your plan toward achieving financial freedom.

Understanding Your Relationship With Money

The way you feel about things makes a huge impact on your attitude toward them. Let me give you an example. If you grew up with the belief that Taco Bell does not make good tacos, no amount of advertisement or actual tacos would be able to completely convince you otherwise. Even if you rationally believe that the tacos are delicious, a small voice in your head will keep telling you, "They're not *that* good."

Your relationship with money works just like that. If you've held certain beliefs all your life, there is a high chance that they are still governing you, even if you don't realize it completely. For instance, a lot of people have a denial about money. When they make a purchase and then receive a "Your account has been debited by $XXX" message, their first instinct is to delete or ignore it. They don't like looking at how much money they have spent or what their account balance is because it freaks them out. Then again, others obsess over money and keep checking the status of their investments and savings multiple times every day. Their world revolves around money, and they associate their self-worth with it.

Exploring the Good and Bad

There can be various forms of beliefs and attitudes toward money which in turn shape how you deal with it. That is why it is very important for you to understand your own perceptions toward money so you can make changes wherever needed.

The entire concept of building a relationship with money can seem quite complicated because it is not something we think about. Sure, we've been taught about having a good relationship with our parents and siblings, and making friends, but nobody really talks about how you should feel about money. As a result, a lot of us have developed an unhealthy mindset toward money which has negatively impacted our financial management endeavors. So, what can you do to fix it?

First things first, let's talk about what it means to have an unhealthy relationship with money. Consider the following scenarios:

- Whenever you feel upset, you buy things to make yourself feel better. It might be in the form of a cheesecake or a new pair of shoes, but it is always some form of impulse shopping.

- You keep using credit cards to buy stuff that you can't afford. For instance, if you are going through an impulse shopping phase, you use your credit card because you don't have that kind of money in your account.

- You don't like managing your money or talking about it, and you keep putting it off until you can't. This also translates to knowing next to nothing about your taxes and how much debt you have.

- You don't like asking for help with your finances even if you know you are struggling. There is a certain level of denial associated with handling monetary issues.

- You feel very anxious while spending money. Even if you are buying necessities, you feel guilty and think it would have been better if you could save this amount.

- You feel angry with people who have money. For instance, when you see people on social media buying new houses or going on European vacations, you feel a sense of rage burning inside you. Basically, you think it is unfair that other people have more money than you, and you're being deprived.

If you identify with even one of these situations (or something close to it), you've got to re-evaluate your relationship with money because you are most definitely suffering from a negative money mindset.

Our money mindset is formed over time and is heavily impacted by our surroundings. Most of the time, it is either something that we have seen while growing up or the complete opposite. The way your parents thought about money also plays a major role in your money mindset. If they were open and had honest financial discussions, there is a higher chance that you wouldn't feel very anxious about money. But since a lot of us grew up in households where talking about money was considered inappropriate, we hold these beliefs close to our hearts and continue to feel intimidated by financial discussions.

Building a Positive Money Mindset

Even though mindset seems like something set in stone, you can easily change it by following a few simple steps and building some good habits. Here are a few pointers that you might find helpful:

- Don't dwell in the past. Life happens, and we make mistakes. But that doesn't mean you have to keep blaming yourself for all the financial missteps you took. Have faith in yourself that you've grown and learned from your mistakes and won't repeat them in the future. If you don't forgive yourself, you'll keep beating yourself up and make no real progress in your financial management journey. It will also make you less confident, and you'll feel anxious every time you make a money decision. Stop the cycle. Learn from the mistake, move on, and believe in yourself.

- Try to understand your financial decisions. Why do you feel the way you feel about money? For instance, you have a habit of delaying all the payments till the last moment. You want to believe that you're making the most out of your money, but sometimes you even miss the due date and end up incurring penalties. Are you really doing this to get the most out of your money, or is it something that you've picked up from your parents or someone close to you? Maybe they had a habit of delaying payments, and you have unconsciously begun to imitate it. If you feel that you have certain problematic financial tendencies, make sure to delve deeper into them. Unless you get to the root cause, you might not be able to modify the behavior.

- Plan your finances and set goals to ensure you are on the right track. Goals give you a sense of direction, and they are a very important aspect of your journey toward achieving financial freedom. We will be talking a lot about budgets and financial planning in this chapter so you can have more clarity on the topic.

- Don't suck the joy out of the financial management process. You can never build a positive mindset toward something that you don't enjoy, which is why it is essential that you feel excited about your finances. Allow yourself to have some fun with your money because you deserve it. Managing your money does not mean you're depriving yourself of all the good things in life, it's just a way to keep things under control and ensure that you're on the right track.

- Don't compare yourself with others because everyone has a different financial journey. I understand that it might feel a bit frustrating to see others having fun while you're struggling, but that is no reason to feel bitter about them. If you are holding a grudge, it's you who will be suffering. Focus on your own goals and financial journey instead of making comparisons. It will protect your peace of mind, and you'll be able to feel more positive about money.

Identifying the Negative Thought Patterns That Might Hinder Financial Progress

Even if you have the best of intentions, building a positive money mindset and staying on top of your financial goals can be quite challenging. Most people tend to deviate from their plans within the first few days, which in turn reinstates the mentality that they are not good with money. It is almost like a vicious cycle and needs to be avoided at all costs. The key here is to identify the negative thought patterns that might be derailing you from your goals and work on improving them. Let's look at some of these common behaviors and how you can stop them from hindering your financial progress.

- **Lack of planning:** When you're just starting something new, you have to keep doing it every day for a while so you can create a habit. You have to create a well-defined plan so you can easily follow through. If you're not creating a budget and making financial plans, there is a high chance that you'll end up making impulse purchases and deviating from your goals. Before diving headfirst into the process, make sure you have adequately planned how you'll execute it.

- **Improper goal setting:** Even if you have been actively setting goals and working on them, you can hinder your financial journey if those goals are not realistic. For instance, if you wish to lose weight and you start following a diet where you only eat broccoli and kale, you won't be able to keep it up. Sure, you'll lose some weight quickly, but then your cravings will take over, and you'll mess up the whole effort. Just like you need a well-balanced diet to keep you healthy, you'll need to set realistic financial goals that will help you stay on top of your finances. An example of healthy financial goals can look like a balanced allocation between savings and investments and allowing yourself to indulge once in a while.

- **Lack of knowledge:** Ignorance about finances can severely hinder your financial progress because unless you know it, you'd never be able to master it. Financial illiteracy is a major problem for most young Americans because most of them have never had any form of financial education in their schools, colleges, or even from their parents. To get over this hindrance, start educating yourself and mastering the basics of financial management.

- **Impatience:** When you plant a seed, do you expect it to bear fruits the next day? No, right? So, it is unrealistic to expect all your money problems to go away immediately after you start your financial management journey. Impatience can be fatal when you're trying to achieve your money goals, so be gentle and patient with yourself as you figure things out.

- **Lack of discipline:** Mastering money skills needs a lot of discipline and consistently directed efforts. To build good money habits, you have to keep at it even when things are not going your way, or you're feeling frustrated. It's not about one isolated event of impulse shopping, it's about addressing the mentality that tempts you to make the purchase.

- **Procrastination:** Putting things off and being in denial about money is one of the major reasons that can hinder your financial progress. Dedicate some time every day to financial planning and tracking your budget.

- **Resistance to change:** Setting financial goals and getting on a path to master money skills can be overwhelming at first, and you might feel that a lot is changing in your life. Do not resist this change and instead try to embrace it because it will help you manage your finances better.

All of these negative thought patterns can contribute to a severe lack of creativity and poor financial decision-making. You have a very unique set of needs from your financial goals, and you've got to find the most creative ways that motivate you to stay aligned with these goals. Good decision-making becomes so much easier when you are enjoying the process because you're already motivated to do the right thing.

Setting Financial Goals

One of the hardest things about beginning a journey toward financial independence is setting goals. You can look up a list of popular financial goals and "things to do" in your 20s or 30s, but it might still not resonate with your requirements. Choosing financial goals that are relevant for you is the most important step in mastering money skills. It all begins with evaluating your current situation and then choosing the best course of action. Irrespective of the other things you wish to achieve financially, here are a few standard goals to start with:

- **Creating a budget:** A budget helps you track your expenses and make a comprehensive plan of spending. So, creating one should be one of the first financial goals that you set for yourself because it will form the foundation for all the other objectives. We will be talking all about budgets and how to create them in the next section of this chapter.

- **Building an emergency fund:** The outbreak of the COVID-19 pandemic is a glaring example of how uncertain life is. Things can suddenly take a turn for the worse, which is why it is very important to start building an emergency fund. Most financial experts are of the opinion that your emergency fund should consist of three to six months of living expenses. Once you have made your budget and know your actual monthly expenses, you can start focusing on building the fund.

- **Building a habit of saving:** You can never go wrong with saving money, so start as soon as you can. Even though the importance of savings is well-established, you might still find it hard to save money at first. Make it automatic, use separate accounts, and do everything else that it takes but start building a savings habit. It will help you tremendously as your finances grow more complex.

- **Controlling spending:** When you're trying to save money and achieve financial goals, you've got to curb overspending and maintain discipline about the money you're earning. Overspending can quickly become a bad habit that you're unable to get rid of. That is why your budget will play a major role in keeping track of your expenses and ensuring you are not going above the specified limit.

- **Planning for retirement:** Even if you are still in your teens or twenties, you should start planning and saving for your retirement. When you have a lot of time, your investments get the benefit of compounding, and your money increases phenomenally. Direct a part of your savings toward retirement and gradually build it so that it doesn't feel like too much pressure.

- **Getting out of credit card debt:** Credit cards are the highest-interest-bearing debts, and they can eat up your savings in no time. While using credit cards can be convenient, you've got to keep it to a minimum and pay your dues on time every month. The interest accumulation will soon be out of control, and you won't be able to manage the debt. We're going to talk a lot about getting out of debt in the next chapter, so don't worry if it sounds overwhelming!

- **Building credit:** You should prioritize building credit right from a young age so that when you're ready to make some big financial decisions, you are prepared and have creditworthiness.

Consider the Time Horizon

Once you have a list of financial goals that you'll be accomplishing, you've got to categorize them according to the time horizon. This is important to ensure that you are focusing on the right goals at the right time. For instance, retirement saving is a long-term goal, while building an emergency fund is an immediate priority. When you are clear about the long- and short-term goals, you can allocate the money accordingly. So, if you feel that you don't have enough money at the moment to dedicate toward all these goals, start with the short-term ones first. It'll give you some confidence, and you'll be taking a step in your journey toward financial freedom. Over time, as your income increases and you have more money to save, you can start contributing more to your long-term goals.

Align Financial Goals With Personal Values

Even though money management seems like a financial concept, there is something inherently personal about it. The way you set your financial goals and the paths you choose to achieve them is closely associated with your mindset. If you keep thinking that "earning and accumulating more money" is your major financial objective, you won't be able to keep yourself motivated. Instead, try to think of the things you wish to achieve with the money you will earn. If you can visualize the life you can lead with financial independence, it will become so much easier for you to follow through with your plans and maintain discipline.

Deep dive into your personal values and the things that truly make you happy. It is important to keep the element of joy in your financial journey so that you don't feel like you are depriving yourself. After all, what is the point of earning money if you cannot have fun at times? Be honest with yourself about your requirements so that you can comfortably achieve your goals. There's no point in comparing yourself with others because you'll only end up messing up your progress. Don't shame yourself for wanting something. Evaluate your wants, and if they are feasible (and affordable), you should definitely work toward achieving them.

Creating a Budget

A budget is one of the most important tools in your financial management journey because it helps you come up with an action plan based on your current income and expense levels. The concept of budgeting has often been perceived as intimidating, which is why many people are plain scared to do it. But if you delve deeper into the actual process and break it down into smaller steps, you'll find it to be one of the simplest things ever.

Understanding the Elements of a Budget

First things first, let's discuss the elements of a budget so that you know what goes into it. All forms of organizations, like governments and corporations, prepare budgets as a part of their financial plans. Although the basic elements are always the same, we will be looking at a personal budget that is made by people to manage their personal expenses. Before you start the actual preparation, it is important to consider a specific time period. Usually, you can consider a month because it is convenient and allows regular progress tracking. Once you've decided on the period, here are the different elements that you'll need to know:

- **Income:** The first step in any budgeting activity is to make a note of your monthly income. If you have multiple sources of income like a job, allowance, and scholarship, make sure to add all of them so you have a clear picture of how much money comes in every month.

- **Estimated expenses:** This is the most critical part of any budget because you need to figure out the different categories of expenses and allocate a specific amount to each one of them. Some examples of expenses include groceries, utilities, rent, gas, and others. If you find this step difficult, take a look at your bank and credit card statements to get insight into how much you are spending and on what. It's important to start somewhere, and you can always make adjustments later on.

- **Actual expenses:** Your budget will also contain the actual expenses that you incur during the month. Write them down and compare them with the estimates so that you know where you might be spending extra or the estimates need modification.

When you are preparing a budget for the first time, you are bound to mess up some of the estimates, but you should consider the rationale behind allocating a certain amount under a particular category. For instance, if you put $200 as your monthly grocery cost, does that mean you think you should spend that much on groceries every month? Or is that simply a random estimate? If you want to get the estimates right, analyze your expenses for a couple of weeks before you start the budgeting process. Even if it feels like you are not doing it right, trust your gut with the estimates.

You might notice that you are going over certain estimates every month but don't beat yourself up if that happens. Instead, take a look at the amount of money you're spending and try to analyze if your estimates are incorrect. For instance, if you feel that you can never buy a month's groceries for $200, check out the prices of all the individual items you are buying. You might find that you need to allocate a greater amount, and that is perfectly fine! Budgeting is not about proving a point, so the figures are not set in stone. If you feel that a certain estimate is not right, feel free to make changes. But remember not to exploit it because you would actually be cheating yourself if you do that.

Creating a Strategy That Works for You

Now that you know the basic structure of a budget and how it works, let's talk about some helpful strategies that you can follow. The main purpose of a budget is to encourage savings and manage your finances efficiently. Here are a few ways to ensure that:

- **50/30/20 budget:** This is a budgeting strategy where you allocate 50% of your total income toward essential expenses, 30% toward wants, and the remaining 20% is saved. The best part about adopting this strategy is that you don't need to dedicate any additional effort toward saving money. You can simply set aside 20% of your income as savings and then decide whatever you wish to do with it. These savings can once again be allocated toward creating emergency funds and achieving other short-term and long-term goals. Since you are also dedicating 30% of your income to your wants or nonessential expenses, you won't be making yourself feel deprived.

- **80/20 budget:** Here, you allocate 20% of your income toward savings, and the other 80% will be spent on everything else. This strategy is also useful for creating savings, but it might become a bit difficult to manage the rest of your expenses. Since you're already setting money aside for savings, you might feel overwhelmed managing all your essential and nonessential expenses in that 80%. So, this strategy is really helpful when you can create accurate estimates for all your spending.

- **Envelope system:** Although this method is a bit old-school, it is still a very effective budgeting strategy for preventing overspending. In this method, you use an envelope for each spending category and allocate a certain amount of money toward it. For instance, if you estimate your monthly grocery expenses to be $300, you'll be putting $300 in your envelope earmarked for groceries. This method helps you stay within your limits for every category and, in turn, maintain the monthly budget.

Even though these strategies are fairly popular, don't feel pressured to follow them blindly. As you get into the habit of preparing budgets, you'll find customized strategies that work for you. They can be a combination of all the above strategies or something that you devised out of your own needs.

Tips for Sticking to a Budget

Preparing a budget is only the tip of the iceberg, and the real difficulty begins when you start following through. Sticking to a budget can seem especially challenging for newbies because you might feel that the budget is restrictive and denying you any breathing space. While these feelings are natural, you've got to get over them to ensure your financial journey goes smoothly. Here are a few time-tested tips that can help you stick to a budget (and feel good about it too):

- **Cover the essentials first:** One of the biggest reasons why people deviate from their budget is because they don't have enough money for their essentials. Once you cover the essential expenses, you'll find it easier to stick to the rest of your budget. For instance, if you're using a 50/30/20 budgeting strategy, set aside that 50% for all your needs right at the beginning of the month. If you're getting paid weekly, then allocate half of that for your essential bills every time.

- **Pay yourself:** After you've covered your bills, make sure you are maintaining your savings rate. Saving more money is one of the primary objectives of budgeting, so it is crucial for you to allocate money for it.

- **Keep a tab on your wants:** Your budget should allow you some breathing space and the scope to have some fun once in a while. That is why keeping a close tab on your "wants" is important. Many people like to skip it and put all their money into savings, thereby depriving themselves of the joy that budgeting can bring them. Over time, they start feeling frustrated and, eventually, end up deviating massively from their budgets because they did not allow themselves the scope to have fun. If you don't have cheat days once in a while, you'll give in to your cravings sooner or later. The same logic applies to budgeting, and you should not push yourself to the point where you are frustrated with the budget. A lot of us have grown up with a mentality where we feel ashamed to indulge ourselves. You need to be kind to yourself and prioritize your wants, too, so that you can easily stick to your budget.

- **Track your progress:** You did all your research about the best strategy according to your financial priorities, but the budget still doesn't seem to be working out for you. I know it's a bit disappointing, but not uncommon. That is why it is very important to track your progress and make sure you're actually able to follow through. At the end of each month, pay close attention to all the areas where your estimates are not matching with the actual expenses to evaluate the differences. Based on your findings, you might either need to modify the budget or try to spend less in that category.

Although "sticking to a budget" sounds very intimidating and grown-up, it's actually nothing more than keeping a close eye on all the individual elements of the budget. You simply have to keep following the strategies that you have already devised for yourself. If you're unable to maintain it for some reason, make adjustments and move on. You can always have a bad month (or two), but the point is to not make it a regular practice to mess up your budget. Your mindset is the most important thing here, and you have to believe in your abilities to follow through.

Reality Checks: Budgeting When You're Poor

Here's a hard pill to swallow: Despite your best intentions to create and stick to a budget, you might find that your income levels are not enough to cover everything that you're budgeting for. But does that mean budgets and financial planning is for "rich" people only? Absolutely not.

If your current income does not seem adequate to include everything in your budget, then you have to make some simple modifications so that it looks more achievable. For starters, prioritize your essential expenses once again so that you don't have to use your credit card too much. Credit card debt carries the highest interest, so you've got to keep it to a minimum. Reduce your savings rate for the time being or until your income increases. There is no point in saving money when you don't have enough to cover your basic necessities.

When you have a low income, the entire focus on your budget should be to stay out of debt and keep the frills to a minimum. Start making meals at home instead of eating out, and that includes your trips to Starbucks too. Make it a point to cut back on all the unnecessary expenses and instead put that money toward building an emergency fund. If you don't have a lot of money coming in, you have to make sure your outflows are also kept at a low level. For example, if you have multiple errands to run, try to get them done on a single day so that you can save on gas money. Cancel a few automatic subscriptions that you don't use regularly, and always keep an eye out for discounts and other promotional offers.

Here, I would also like to include that if you feel that your income isn't enough to at least maintain a 10% savings rate, you should probably look for ways to boost your earnings. Pick up a few overtime shifts if your employer gives you the option to do so, or look for some side gigs to go along with your full-time job. At the end of the day, increasing your income is the only way to ensure you are saving enough money and indulging yourself in your wants. A big part of financial planning is to learn when your income is falling short and what you can do to improve the situation.

Interactive Element

Although there are various tools that you can use to make the budgeting process easier, you can also start your journey with a basic template. Don't worry if you don't know how to make one, we've got you covered! Here is an easy format that you can consult as you start your budgeting journey. It is based on the 50/30/20 budgeting strategy, but you can customize it according to your convenience.

Period of budget: [Enter the name of the month here]

Monthly income		
1	Salaries/wages	$ XXXX
2	Income from a part-time job	$ XXXX
3	Any other source of income/inflow	$ XXXX
	Total income	**$ XXXX**

Expenses for necessities (50% of income)		
1	Food	$ XXXX
2	Rent	$ XXXX
3	Utilities	$ XXXX
4	Transportation	$ XXXX
5	Anything else that is needed for survival	$ XXXX
	Total	**$ XXXX**

Expenses for wants (30%)		
1	Eating out (including coffee)	$ XXXX
2	Subscriptions (gym, streaming platforms, etc.)	$ XXXX
3	Shopping (clothes, books, etc.)	$ XXXX
4	Anything else	$ XXXX
	Total	**$ XXXX**

Savings (20%)		
1	Automated contributions	$ XXXX
2	Any other savings schemes	$ XXXX
3	Any other source of income/inflow	$ XXXX
	Total income	**$ XXXX**

Budgeting Apps to Use

If you find budgeting to be too daunting and don't feel confident in making a template, here are a few budgeting apps that you can use:

- **Mint:** This is one of the most useful budgeting apps for teens and young adults and the best part is that it is completely free for everyone. Mint connects all your bank accounts, credit cards, and even investment accounts and gives you a comprehensive overview of your financial situation. It categorizes expenses into various types that facilitate the budgeting process. You can manage your bills, set reminders, and stay on top of your finances. Mint also has a ton of educational resources that you can consult.

- **You Need a Budget (YNAB):** This is an app for the more serious budgeters who like to have a lot of control over the process. YNAB is a paid app that helps users get out of debt and provides useful financial advice. It is based on the principle of a zero-based budget, which means that all the money will be allocated toward some category, and there won't be anything unused. These strict allocations help the users stay on top of their finances and meet every goal properly.

- **PocketGuard:** This is a basic app that has both free and paid versions. There are budgeting features along with expense categorization and specialized tools to improve savings. PocketGuard has a unique algorithm that tracks all the inflows and outflows and displays the amount of money available to the user for meeting their daily expenses.

- **Empower:** This is a free budgeting tool that comes with an investment management service add-on at an extra cost. It links all your accounts and categorizes expenses into different types, but you can also customize them according to your requirements.

Setting financial goals can feel a bit like dreaming, sort of like when you look at probable destinations and plan for a vacation. But it doesn't feel "real" until you've booked your tickets and confirmed the itinerary. Similarly, to actually realize your dreams of achieving financial independence, you've got to take some real steps, and getting yourself out of debt is the first one. In the next chapter, we will be talking about debt, ways to evaluate it, and important strategies that will help you in reducing it over time.

Chapter 2:

Get Out of Debt

Debt is one person's liability, but another person's asset. –Paul Krugman

Credit card bills. Mortgage payments. Student loan repayment. Is there something else that you're missing? There might be a couple of other debts too, but you can't even remember it properly because it is so overwhelming. If you feel burdened by the implications of debt, then you are definitely not alone. According to a study by Andrew Depietro and Gaby Lapera on behalf of Credit Karma (2023), the average millennial in the USA has $48,611 worth of debt in 2023. That's a lot of money to owe! Now, let's look at some other statistics. The average salary of a millennial is around $47,034, which means that it is highly probable many of them have more debt in comparison to their income (Fries, 2023).

If you're not thinking about getting rid of debt as soon as possible, you are at risk of derailing your entire journey toward achieving financial freedom. That is why, in this chapter, we will break down debt and understand it from a deeper perspective so that it becomes easier for us to evaluate and eventually repay it.

Evaluating Your Debt

The best way to get a grip on something is by knowing it really well, and the same goes for debt. A major reason why so many people struggle with debt is that they do not understand what each type of loan entails or what they're dealing with. There's a lot of ignorance about debt, and the lack of financial education simply aggravates the issue. Most of us are handed a pile of debt before we even know what's going on, and by the time we realize it, we are already burdened by its weight and too busy to manage it.

Types of Debt

The best way to break the cycle of debt weighing you down is to understand the types of debt and how they might be affecting your finances. Debt can be categorized into the following types:

- **Secured:** This is a type of debt that is secured by some asset that you own. This asset is used as a pledge to back up the debt that you have undertaken, and in the event of a default, the lender can seize the asset and foreclose the loan. The amount of debt is usually determined by the value of the asset that you are pledging. Auto loans and mortgages are examples of secured debt. Since these loans are secured by an asset, the rate of interest charged is lower.

- **Unsecured:** Unlike secured debt, there is no apparent "security" for unsecured debts which means no assets are pledged as a part of this loan. The lender would usually check the borrower's creditworthiness and financial condition before approving the loan to ensure they have the capacity to repay. Credit cards and personal loans are examples of unsecured debt. Since there is an underlying risk of the loan not being repaid, the borrowers charge higher rates of interest for unsecured debt.

- **Revolving:** The borrower gets a limit or a line of credit from which they can borrow, and as long as they are repaying it (or a specified minimum amount) within the due dates, they can keep maintaining the limit. Credit cards work on revolving credit, where you can spend up to a certain limit and pay your bills every month. Revolving debt is essentially unsecured, so the rate of interest is some of the highest.

- **Mortgages:** This is a type of secured loan that is exclusively related to buying a house. People who wish to buy houses usually take a mortgage where the lender would provide a certain percentage of the total price of the house. In most cases, the borrower would also come up with an upfront payment to complete the purchase. For instance, the buyer can pay for 20% of the house and take out a mortgage for the remaining 80%.

Calculating How Much You Owe

When you take out a loan, the lender is going to charge interest at a certain rate as the reward for the risk they are undertaking. Debts that have a higher rate of interest are more difficult to pay off because the interest accumulation increases the actual amount due. That is why you've got to stay on top of your borrowing and actually know how much money you owe. Calculating the actual balances due can be daunting, which is why you should consider using an online debt tracker. You simply have to enter the details of each type of debt (like amount, rate of interest, repayment period, monthly installment amounts, etc.), and the tracker will calculate their position at the end of each month.

Good vs. Bad Debt

When you're evaluating your loans, you need to understand the difference between good and bad debt. Now you must be thinking, how can debt be good? Well, it turns out, even though debt has a very negative image in personal finance, not all of it is actually bad for you. The loans that you take for buying assets like a house or a car are not considered to be bad debts because these assets are regarded as investments. Think of it this way—a house provides you with a place to live, and once the loan is repaid, you'll own the asset. The house can also provide you with a sense of security and can be used as collateral if you need another loan in the future. The same goes for auto loans—a car can help you get to places where public transportation might not be available. Student loans are also considered to be good debts because investing in your education is one of the best things you can do for your future.

The debts that are undertaken for purchasing consumer goods are usually regarded as bad. For instance, credit card debt is always considered to be bad because most people use credit cards for purchasing things for regular use. Personal loans and other high-interest debts are also bad. If you have large amounts of credit card debt, it can be quite challenging to repay it because of the high-interest rates. These debts are bad for your financial health because they hinder any progress that you might have made while managing your personal finances. The repayments can add up, and you might not be able to save any money or allocate funds toward your financial goals. Keeping your bad debts in check is the key to smoothening the path toward financial freedom.

Strategies for Debt Repayment

The truth about debt is that if you are not managing it properly, it can quickly wreak havoc in your personal finance journey. While debt is unavoidable at times, you should also make it a priority to start devising repayment strategies right from the beginning. Although it sounds like the job of an expert, you can easily do it too! Here are some tried and tested methods that you can follow to gradually get out of debt and achieve financial freedom.

P.S. Before you start going through the debt repayment strategies, make sure you are setting aside money for making additional repayments.

Debt Snowball

This is the first and most common debt repayment strategy, where you focus on repaying the smallest debts first, irrespective of their interest rate. To do that, you have to first categorize your debts from smallest to largest, based on the amount due. Then dedicate your budgeted amount for extra repayment toward the smallest debts. The logic behind this method is that if you focus on the smaller debts, you'll be able to tackle the repayments faster. It might not always make sense financially because the smallest debt isn't always the one that has the highest interest. But the debt snowball method gives a sense of confidence and helps you believe that you are capable of repaying your debts. It is also quicker in terms of achieving your repayment goals.

Let us look at it with the help of a numerical example. Suppose your budget allows you to dedicate an additional $200 toward debt repayments over and above the minimum amounts due for each loan. You have the following dues:

	Name of the debt	Rate of interest	Total amount due	Minimum amount due every month
1	Mortgage	6.65%	$259,556	$5,175
2	Credit card	22%	$5,750	$521
3	Hospital bill	NA	$860	$215
4	Auto loan	7%	$19,258	$1,498

In such a case, you'd first look at repaying the hospital bill because it is the smallest debt you have. So, you'd pay $415 ($200 + $215) every month toward the hospital bill so that it is repaid first. Since it is a small debt, you'll be able to meet it completely within three months and then move on to the next one, which would be a credit card in this case.

Debt Avalanche

The biggest problem of using the debt snowball method is that while you're repaying the smaller debts, the high-interest ones can actually increase your total amount due. If you feel like you can take on the bigger debts and are ready to dive head-first into the process, the debt avalanche method will be more suitable for you. This method targets the highest-interest debts first and gradually moves on to the lower-interest ones. The benefit is that you will be dedicating your extra money toward the most expensive loans, which would, in turn, helps you save money in the long run. If you consider the table in the previous section, you'll start with the credit card debt under the debt avalanche method.

Even though it is an effective way to ensure your expensive debts are not weighing you down, the debt avalanche method can be difficult to manage for beginners. Since you're tackling high-interest debts first, it might take you longer to repay them, which in turn can become demotivating. It also requires a lot of discipline and probably won't work if you don't have a steady income source. That is why many people fail to follow through even though this method is technically ideal in terms of repaying debts and saving money.

Combination of Both Debt Snowball and Avalanche

Both debt snowball and avalanche methods have their own share of pros and cons, which is why you should consider mixing them up in your debt repayment journey. There is no strict rule that you have to follow one method rigidly. Life changes and so do our priorities and outlook toward financial management. Taking on high-interest debts might seem intimidating in your late teens or early twenties, but that doesn't mean you'll feel the same way when you reach your thirties.

Start with the method that resonates with your current financial situation, and don't go overboard. Repaying your debts isn't your only financial commitment, and you also have to remember to budget for your basic necessities.

The debt snowball method can be a good place to start your debt repayment journey because it is simple and takes less effort. Once you have successfully repaid the smallest debt, you can take a moment to bask in the glory of your achievement. Repaying one debt will help you get acquainted with the process, and then you can move on to the debt avalanche method. The endgame is to free yourself of debt as soon as you can, so you are allowed to use any methods that work for you.

Negotiating With Creditors to Restructure Debt

At times, things don't work out according to plan, and you might fall behind in making repayments. In such a case, you are at risk of damaging your credit score and incurring heavy penalties unless you can take some conclusive strategy to get yourself out of the mess. Debt consolidation and restructuring can be a good option when you're struggling to manage your debts and unable to make the full repayment on time. This is a process where you negotiate with the creditors for better loan terms like a lower rate of interest or a bigger repayment period.

The first thing to do when you're struggling with your debts is to take a hard look at your budget and look for areas where you can cut back. You'd be amazed at how small expenses can add up and create problems when trying to manage your finances. Once you've explored all the options to make things better, I'd suggest you evaluate how much you can actually afford to repay. Your situation might be better (or worse) than you imagined, which is why it is crucial to be sure about the numbers. Your creditors might look for a lump sum payment instead of regular reduced installments, so make sure you can afford that too. Book an appointment with your creditors and let them know about your situation. Have a strategy right from the beginning and keep your offers lower than what you can actually afford. It is a sensitive discussion, and you need to make the creditors understand your situation. That is why it's important to maintain a professional tone and not express any kind of dissatisfaction if they don't agree. If you can convince the creditor to get your debts settled, you must remember to ask for a written agreement that confirms the new terms of the loan. This will protect you from any unprecedented legal issues later on. It might seem detrimental to your finances to hire a lawyer for an agreement but trust me, it'll be worth it. You can also speak with a credit counselor to understand your financial situation better and make a more suitable offer to the creditors.

Another way of dealing with debt settlements is hiring a debt settlement company to do it for you. These companies typically charge a fee for the service, but they will save you a lot of time in the process. Debt settlement can be lengthy, and doing it yourself might not always be feasible, especially if you have a very busy work schedule.

Debt settlement can come in various forms, like balance transfers or a consolidated loan and can be a very useful tool while you try to navigate your finances. It can also prevent you from filing for bankruptcy which is the last resort in cases of financial distress. You should note that if you opt for credit settlement, it will have a negative impact on your credit score. But remember, you can always improve your credit score once you have fixed up your financial situation. If you feel like you are struggling with your finances, do not hesitate to opt for debt settlement.

Ways to Avoid Future Debt

One of the best ways to avoid being burdened by debt is to figure out why you have so much of it in the first place. As mentioned earlier, some forms of debt are unavoidable. For instance, if you're planning to buy a house, you would need to take out a mortgage because usually, people don't have that kind of cash available. But if you're careful with your spending decisions and lifestyle choices, you might be able to avoid being trapped by debt. Some of the most common reasons why people end up in a lot of debt are low income, high credit card usage, the burden of unexpected expenses, and spending too much on maintaining a flashy lifestyle.

Maintaining a Debt-Free Lifestyle

As a responsible adult, you've got to address the issues at the root so they don't blow out of proportion later on. Right from the time you start your journey toward financial freedom and become more aware of money management, you have to pay close attention to your debt situation. Budgeting and keeping track of your expenses are the first steps, but you also need a more systematic approach. Here are a few helpful tips that you can follow to use credit efficiently and eventually maintain a debt-free lifestyle.

- The first and most important thing is to keep your spending levels lower than your income. Refer back to the 50/30/20 budgeting strategy, where you dedicate 50% of your income toward all your basic expenses and 30% toward wants. Having a well-structured budgeting strategy will help you prevent overspending and build accountability toward your actions. It might seem like a very obvious thing, but a lot of people struggle to keep their expenses under control and end up borrowing money to pay the bills. By the time they have repaid one of their loans, there is more that gets piled up, creating a debt trap.

- Life is uncertain and unexpected events can easily derail you from your financial goals. For instance, if you suddenly fall sick or have an accident, you might not be able to work at your full capacity, which in turn can cause a dent in your income streams. In such cases, your finances are bound to take a turn for the worse because you'll have to meet the additional expenses that have come up because of this unexpected situation. This is when you might start using your credit card for all your expenses because there isn't enough money to meet the basic expenses. That is why it is absolutely crucial to have an emergency fund that can help you until you can get back on your feet. The emergency fund can also save you from using your credit card or taking on other forms of debt.

- Even though car loans are not always considered to be "bad," they still fall under the category of consumer debt. A car is a highly depreciable asset which means that its value will go down by at least 20% (or more, depending on usage) in the first year itself (Ramsey Solutions, 2023). Instead of spending a ton of money and taking out a big loan to buy an expensive car, consider purchasing a second-hand vehicle or even renting one. If public transport is easily available in your area, consider using it instead of a car. Car loan payments can add up, and it can take you a long time to repay it. You might still be paying on a loan for a car that has completely depreciated.

- Prevent overspending by becoming a value-based spender. This doesn't mean that you can't buy things you want or indulge yourself once in a while. But you should be making smart spending decisions and avoiding impulse shopping as much as you can. While retail therapy can give you that momentary serotonin boost, it can be quite catastrophic for your finances if you don't keep it in check. Impulse buying is one of the biggest contributors to credit card debt because these are the things that you haven't budgeted for. Think about it, you have a budget, and you're really committed to following it. But you had a really bad day at work, and you're lying sleepless on your bed at 1 a.m. when you receive a notification from your favorite shopping app. You open it, without any intention of buying anything, but as you're virtual window shopping, you find that a pair of your wishlisted running shoes are on sale. Even after the sale discount, the price is more than you had allocated for your "wants," but you are tempted to buy them. After a few moments of hesitation, you decide to buy them because you feel you deserve to treat yourself after the day you've had. Since you don't have the money in your account, using a credit card is the only way to buy those shoes. Even if you don't relate to this particular situation, things like these happen all the time and increase your credit card debt. Create some ground rules to ensure you are not overspending. For instance, if it exceeds your monthly allocated amount for "wants," don't buy it. Or, if you cannot afford to pay for it with a debit card, don't buy it. Putting a check on overspending is the only way to ensure you are not overusing your credit cards and maintaining a healthy financial balance.

- Speaking of credit cards, make sure that you are repaying them as soon as you can. Keep your credit card expenses at a minimum, and make sure you're paying the entire amount every month. Try not to enter into the loop of making minimum payments because the interest can add up and cause the debt to increase phenomenally. Credit card interest rates can be around 20% or even more which means that if you have $1000 due, it will become $1,200 next month. In case you are unable to make more than the minimum payment, don't make more purchases on your credit card so that you are not adding up to the debt. It is also important to keep the number of credit lines at a minimum. Once you've got the first card, you'll keep getting calls from other credit card companies. They will offer you a better card with a higher limit and other unique benefits. Even though it can be tempting, remember the implications it might have when you're trying to repay your high-interest debts. Managing ten credit cards is much harder than managing only two—it's simple math. If you already have more than five cards, start closing them out one by one so that you can control your spending habits.

- A big part of becoming debt-free is making certain choices, even if you don't feel like it. For instance, you can't say yes to every social occasion or each time your friends ask you to accompany them going out. Your choices can make a huge difference in how you deal with your finances and, in turn, how much debt you take on. Your lifestyle needs to resonate with your financial goals. If you make it a priority to repay debts and then you go hang out with your friends four times a week at expensive places, you won't be able to follow through with your debt repayment plans.

Becoming debt-free isn't something you'll achieve in a short time span, so you should be patient with yourself in this journey. If you start with a debt snowball strategy, you will take longer to make a dent in your bigger debts, and if you follow a debt avalanche strategy, it might take you years before you can fully repay your highest-interest debts. You'll find plenty of debt-repayment stories where the borrowers have successfully managed to repay all their loans and are now living a happy life. While these stories can be very inspiring, they can also make you feel like you're not doing enough. It is very easy to fall into the loop of self-blame and criticism even when you are taking all the necessary steps. Always remember, the stories you read on social media are not the full picture. Everyone has a different financial journey, and if you compare yourself with others, you'll only end up adding to your frustration. Choose the repayment strategies that work best for you, and don't follow anyone else's advice blindly. You might need to modify some strategies based on your unique requirements. If you truly feel that you need further guidance, consider speaking with a consultant who can help you by providing credit counseling and managing your finances.

Track Your Progress and Celebrate the Wins

Debt repayment and maintaining a debt-free lifestyle can turn out to be a difficult task, especially when you are trying to build a habit of it. That is why you've got to keep monitoring your progress to ensure you are on the right track. Repaying your debts will require a lot of discipline and some sacrifice. Keeping yourself motivated can be a challenge when you have to give up things you enjoy which is why you should always celebrate the small wins and reward yourself. For instance, when you manage to successfully repay your first small debt, make sure you treat yourself with something. Spending money on yourself while trying to repay debts might seem contradictory, but it's important to keep your spirits high on this journey.

Getting out of debt is actually a matter of huge focus and commitment. You'll have to stick to the budgeting rules and go through all the plans that you make to improve your finances. It is going to take a mental toll on you, which is why it is important to have a positive attitude toward money in general. Building a positive money mindset is probably one of the most important steps you can take to ease your financial journey. In the next chapter, we'll be talking about your attitude toward money and how you can get into a wealth mindset to avoid the common financial mistakes that most people make.

Chapter 3:

An Attitude for Money

A wise person should have money in their head, but not in their heart. –
Jonathan Swift

As a child, I remembered my parents teaching me lessons like "money can't buy happiness" or "money isn't everything." But as a teenager, these lessons had little meaning, especially when I felt I never had any money to afford anything. You see, I was still living with my parents and only had a part-time job at a local diner. Naturally, I did not have enough money for a lot of things, and that often led to frustrations and the feeling of "I'm not good enough without any money." Unconsciously, I was building a negative money mindset. These feelings got stronger during the holidays when we used to have a big family gathering every year, and some of my really rich relatives would come to visit. One of those cousins, Chad, would always act like he was better than everyone and would go out of their way to be mean. Of course, we were all kids back then, but I understood that it was because his family had a lot of money that paved the way for such arrogance. Chad would behave as if it was okay to do all sorts of wrong things and get away with it. As an angry teen, I would often have two extreme kinds of emotions about money:

1. Money is the root cause of all evil.

2. Money is the only thing that matters in life.

Eventually, I figured out that none of the above statements were true, but it took me a while to internalize a positive money mindset. I also realized the way Chad behaved was actually not uncommon. There are numerous studies that point out the adverse effects of money on morality and the way people perceive their relationships. San Francisco has a law that cars have to stop at crosswalks so that pedestrians can pass. According to a UC Berkeley study, drivers of luxury cars were four times less likely to follow this law and stop their cars in comparison to drivers of other regular cars (Gregoire, 2018). This is a clear indication of rich people caring less about others and thinking it was okay not to follow the law because they could get away with it.

While money has a lot of power to make or break things, you need to ensure that you're not attaching your entire sense of self-worth to how much money you have. Most of us are so busy chasing after money, we forget to take a moment and evaluate how we actually feel about it. Does it bother us? Do we feel comfortable talking about it? Until you are sure about your feelings, you'll find it very difficult to feel confident in your money management journey. That is why, in this chapter, we will be talking about how you can build a healthier attitude toward money, get into a wealth mindset, and truly become a master of your finances.

Change Your Attitude About Money

Before getting further into the discussion, let us first talk about what a money mindset actually entails. It is a unique set of attitudes and beliefs that you develop over time. Like most other things, your surroundings and upbringing play a major role in how you feel about money. Let us look at a couple of examples:

- As a child, Sarah always saw both her parents actively participate in financial discussions. It was a weekly thing when her mom and dad would sit at the dinner table with a pen and paper and make a list of all the expenses that they had. At times, things got tough, and she'd hear her parents say things like, "We need to cut back a bit," but there was never any major negative emotion associated with it. Words like these meant simple dinners for the week, and mom wouldn't allow her to buy any additional candy while grocery shopping. Although they did not actively involve her in the monetary discussions, they never discouraged Sarah from listening or following the money rules of the house. When she asked for money to buy something, her parents would always rationalize it for her. If it was too expensive, Sarah's mom would tell her it's not something they can afford at the moment and suggest the next best thing. So, once she grew up, money wasn't a daunting element in her life. Sure, she struggled with it a lot during her college days and before landing a job, but Sarah knew all she had to do was cut back. She followed the rules of simple meals and even felt encouraged to discuss finances with her partner because that's what she had seen growing up.

- Jane's story was a bit different. She used to be Sarah's neighbor as a child, and both of them belonged to a similar financial background. But Jane's family was a bit more orthodox, and it was only her dad who took care of all the finances. There wasn't really much discussion around money, and whenever she would ask for money, it was always met with anger and words like, "You can buy it when you earn money yourself." Jane found it harder to tackle money once she moved out for college because she was never a part of any financial discussions at home. In fact, she never remembered her parents having any kind of discussion about money. Once she started earning her own money, she would often indulge herself by making impulse purchases because she was deprived of the things she wanted while growing up.

Jane and Sarah grew up with very different attitudes toward money, which is bound to reflect in their financial mindset too. While Sarah has a relatively healthier money mindset, Jane often gives in to her impulsive spending tendencies because she thinks it's okay to spend the money she has earned on things she wants. There's absolutely nothing wrong in indulging yourself, but if you're doing that every time you want to blow off some steam, it might soon turn into a problem.

You might not have a lot of control over how you were brought up or how your surroundings impacted your money mindset, but you can always take steps now to unlearn the problematic things and build a healthier relationship with money.

Know Your Money Personality Type

The first step toward creating a positive money mindset is to understand your financial personality. Our emotions play a major role in determining how we feel about money which is why only educating yourself about the different financial products will not do the trick. Here are seven money personality types that experts have identified after conducting in-depth research about money personality (Honda, 2021). You might find that you fall under multiple categories, and that is perfectly fine! Life is always changing, and our attitude toward everything is affected by our current situations.

1. **Compulsive saver:** This is a person who likes to save as much money as they can without possibly spending any of it. Although saving is a great habit, compulsive savers don't have proper financial goals, they are simply saving because they feel it is the only thing to do with money. Compulsive savers often tend to be unhappy and have a negative money mindset because they do not indulge themselves at all.

2. **Compulsive spender:** These people usually spend more than they can afford and might often be considered extremely generous. They like to spend money on themselves and others, often without any apparent reason. Compulsive spenders do not have a healthy relationship with money because whenever they are feeling happy or sad, their only outlet for these emotions lies in impulse spending.

3. **Compulsive moneymaker:** These are people who feel that making more money is the only important thing in life and hustle as much as they can to increase their earnings. Since they make it a point to earn a lot of money, they usually do not face financial issues but tend to develop an unhealthy obsession where they feel money is the only good thing in life. Similar to compulsive savers, they might never spend any of the money they have earned.

4. **Indifferent to money:** These people are usually rich and don't have to think a lot about money in their daily lives. That is why they are very indifferent to money and their finances in general, which can often make

them careless too. When we talk about this money personality type, we think of people who are born into wealth.

5. **Saver-Splurger:** This personality type is a combination of savers and spenders, where people save a lot of money and then tend to lose most of it during one of their spending sprees. Even though they prepare budgets and try to accomplish their financial goals, their impulse spending habits can wreak havoc in their journey.

6. **Gambler:** These people are risk lovers who believe that undertaking high-stakes investment or business ventures are the only way to make a lot of money. They might earn millions and lose it all in a single risky streak. Even though gamblers often belong to a high-income bracket, they are reckless about their financial decisions.

7. **Worrier:** This is the most common money personality type, and most people tend to exhibit some of its traits. True to their name, worriers are always worried about not having enough money. They are anxious about their income levels, savings rate, and their overall financial situation, even if there is not much to worry about. Their negative emotions toward money often prevent them from making rational financial decisions and living up to their full potential.

Understanding your money personality type is a very important step because it will help you identify the problems that you might encounter. For instance, if you are a saver-splurger, your savings rate will suffer unless you can put a check on your impulse spending habits. On the other hand, if you are a combination of compulsive moneymaker and compulsive saver, there is a high chance of never feeling happy despite having a lot of money. Striking a balance is essential for a healthy money mindset.

Identifying Negative Beliefs and Behaviors

Once you've identified your money personality type, you need to start focusing on the various negative beliefs and behaviors that you might have developed over time. We often form habits unconsciously based on the events and situations occurring around us. My dad believed firmly that because he was not obese, he did not need to exercise at all. This belief grew from the way he was brought up because my grandparents thought the same too. He was fine when he was younger because he was generally active, but in his late 30s, he started developing gut issues, and the doctor suggested he exercise at least four times a week. Dad was forced to unlearn his belief because of his health issues, but you don't have to wait for something *that* severe to happen before you can change your money mindset.

I get it, it's not easy to figure out where you might be going wrong with your financial attitude, especially if you've never consciously thought about it. So, let's start with some common negative thoughts people tend to have about money and see how many of them resonate with you.

- *I don't have enough money to do anything.* This is probably one of the most common money-related emotions where people feel that they don't have money for any of the things needed to achieve financial freedom. For instance, they cannot save, invest, plan for retirement, buy things they want, or lead a happy life because they don't have the money to do so. This also gives rise to further negative thoughts like I am not good enough, my life is horrible, or I never get what I want.

- *Money is the root of all evil.* I personally know this too well because there was a time in my teens when I strongly felt this emotion. People who feel money causes all problems are usually the ones who feel overwhelmed while handling it. If they have too much of it, they end up overspending, and if they don't have enough, they feel their needs are not being met.

- *I won't ever be rich because I wasn't born into wealth.* These people feel life hasn't been fair to them because they were not born into wealth. They have a lot of struggle, and a part of them have often given up even before they actually start the process of financial management. They also hold a lot of anger toward the rich and feel that rich people have all the benefits in the world.

- *I don't have a fancy college degree, so I will never understand money stuff.* These people feel concepts like investing and saving are too hard for them to understand since they don't have any formal education in this field. Because of that, they also tend to shy away from educating themselves too.

These are just some of the negative emotions that are commonly associated with money and financial management. I'm sure there are more, but I think you get the point.

Changing the Perspective

Building a negative money mindset was probably not your choice. Maybe you heard your parents say these statements over and over during your childhood, or maybe your situation made you look at things in a certain way. We all have our reasons for behaving the way we do, but as responsible human beings, we should also try to address the negative feelings and work on them so that they do not cause hindrances in our journey. That is exactly what we're going to do with all the adverse emotions associated with money and turn them around so you can view them from a fresh perspective.

Identify your negative thoughts and try to figure out why you have them. I know it's easier said than done, but we've got to start somewhere. For instance, if you feel that you don't have enough money and that is ruining your life, analyze the emotion step-by-step.

- How much money do you actually have? If you are already earning and have a stable income, then calculating the total receipt per month can be a good place to start. If you're still a full-time student and don't have a proper job yet, then you should probably not blame yourself for not having enough money. You wouldn't blame a seedling that has just been planted for not bearing fruits already, would you?

- Now think about the "why" behind the emotion. Why do you feel the lack of money is ruining your life? Do you want a particular thing and don't have the money to buy it? Or is it something else? There is a high probability that you might be upset over something else which is causing you to spiral. If you can think of something that you're unable to afford at the moment, don't beat yourself up! You probably have other commitments that you need to take care of, which is why you can't allocate the money for that particular want. Think about all the good things you're doing with the money you have. Maybe you are taking care of your family, covering your necessities, or paying for other stuff. If you're not earning yet, you are devoting your time toward your education, which would help you make money in the future. Either way, you're not ruining your life and doing the best you can, given the current circumstances.

- If you're feeling bad about being unable to afford something, set a goal with a specific timeline to achieve it. For instance, if you want to buy a new laptop that costs $1,000, look at your budget to figure out how much you can dedicate money each month toward buying it.

Whenever you are feeling that money is the main reason behind your problems, take a step back and evaluate the problems that you are talking about. Achieving financial stability is not something that happens in a day. Even people who are "born into wealth" had a predecessor who did the hard work. Instead of getting mad at the rich, think of yourself as the first in your family who will break the cycle of poverty and take a step to improve their finances. You've got to stay committed to the process and make sure you're doing everything you can to overcome the challenges. Shifting your perspective about money is not easy, but it's the only way to develop a positive attitude and stay focused on your journey.

Once you really delve deeper into the emotions that affect your money psychology, you'll be exposed to your own fears and discomforts. Don't give up, because it only gets easier from there. You'll identify the causes behind your feelings and gain clarity about your actions. This is also the key to getting comfortable with your priorities and taking active steps to live life on your own terms. People try very hard to fit themselves into societal norms and follow bucket lists that have no connection with their life. Think about it, if you have clinically diagnosed vertigo, would you want to go bungee jumping? No, right? Because it can be potentially life-threatening and cause a lot of harm to you. So, why would you follow someone else's financial goals and try to mold yourself according to popular standards? You don't have to meet your soulmate by 25, go on European vacations every year, or do everything on the "30 things to do before turning 30" list. Think of all the awesome things you are doing with your life and pat yourself on the back.

The Wealth Mindset

There's a popular saying that states, "Money screams but wealth whispers." For the longest time, I found it to be a very confusing statement because differentiating between money and wealth isn't an easy feat. Right from the time we start our journey toward financial freedom, we tend to confuse the two terms because the common notion is that being rich always translates to being wealthy. But if you look deeper into the concepts of financial management, you'll realize that they are not the same. In fact, a lot of people who seem to be rich are not wealthy at all.

Suppose a person makes around $400,000 a year and naturally belongs to the elite group of very high-income individuals. As expected, they have a very flashy lifestyle. They drive an expensive car, live in a penthouse, and have another vacation house near the beach where they spend their leisure time. Despite making so much money and falling under the so-called "rich" category, they are burdened with consumer debt thanks to their high standard of living. These people are only rich, but not wealthy because they are spending their entire income to maintain their lifestyle. It's not only unnecessary but also makes little financial sense. Since all their money is being spent, they would not be able to build an income stream for the future and subsequently derail the wealth-creation process.

Being wealthy is a bigger concept than being rich. A wealthy person focuses on saving their money, making smart investments, and creating a revenue-generating asset so that even if they are not making any money at any point in their lives, they will always be taken care of. Basically, wealthy people are forward-thinking and try to create adequate financial provisions for their future. They are prepared for whatever might come, which is why they are unperturbed by emergencies or any other unexpected events.

Right from the time you start earning money and get on a path to achieve financial freedom, you should aim to develop a wealth mindset. Making a lot of money won't make a huge difference in your life unless you learn the methods of creating wealth. Building a positive money mindset will help you resonate with the concept of wealth, and you'll see for yourself why it is a good idea to save money for the future instead of a flashy lifestyle in the present.

Strategies for Building a Wealth Mindset

Building a wealth mindset needs conscious efforts and dedication because it is very easy to get swayed by distractions. Here are a few helpful strategies that can help you to create and get into a wealth mindset:

- **Have a plan:** Setting financial goals and following your budget is one of the primary strategies that you need to follow to build a wealth mindset. You should be clear about what you want and how you plan to execute it because it will give you confidence in your finances.

- **Prioritize time:** Even if you are just a student and don't have a lot going on, learn to prioritize your time. As you grow older, you'll realize that time is one of the most valuable assets, and you need to protect it at all costs. Wealthy people are choosy about how they spend their time so that they can devote their attention to the things that matter. Master time management by adding everything to your calendar and staying on top of everything that's been happening.

- **Spend to earn more:** The key to creating wealth is to build income-generating assets. Wealthy people do not shy away from spending money when they need to. But they tend to save and invest in assets that will help them earn more money in the future. For instance, instead of buying an expensive phone, they will spend the money by purchasing stocks of a growing company. The phone will become useless in a couple of years, but the stock will fetch them more money in the form of dividends and capital appreciation.

- **Get into a benefit mindset:** A benefit mindset is one where you volunteer to help others and find a sense of purpose in your life and financial plans. You don't have to be an expert to lend a helping hand, but the act of assisting others and providing a benefit to them can help you grow in your journey. Creating wealth has a lot to do with building a supportive ecosystem for everyone around you so that they can grow with you too.

Financial Mistakes to Avoid

Getting into a wealth mindset is probably one of the hardest things on your personal finance journey. You have to be careful about how you deal with the money you earn and the decisions you make to ensure your actions resonate with your desire to create wealth. Here are some of the top financial mistakes that you need to avoid to fulfill your dream:

- Spending too much money on everyday things will make it impossible for you to get into a wealth mindset. Of course, it feels fancy to buy the expensive cheese for your charcuterie board or drive a luxury car, but think about the turn your finances will take if you keep making these decisions. Like I keep emphasizing, it is always okay to indulge yourself once in a while, but overspending should not be your entire life's mantra. This includes spending money on others as well. I'm not asking you to be cheap, but if you have a big social circle, make sure you're spending money on them wisely. You don't have to get expensive gifts for all of them on their birthdays or always show up with fancy chocolates or wines to house parties. Prioritize your expenses and keep overspending at bay to build a healthier relationship with money and, in turn, create wealth.

- Even though life can sometimes become really busy, you need to remember to pay all your bills on time. If you delay, you are at risk of ruining your credit score and incurring extra expenses in the form of fines and penalties. One of the biggest conditions of building wealth is that you can never be careless about money. Even if it's a tiny bill, you need to ensure you're paying it within the due date.

- I've said this before, and I'll say it again: Don't compare your life with others and let their decisions influence yours. Follow your own plans and do whatever it takes to stay on track. Spending too much to maintain an image on social media will cost you more than just money. A large part of getting into a wealth mindset is getting comfortable in your space and doing life your own way.

- Wealthy people are well-informed, and they always like to get their money's worth. To get into a wealth mindset, you have to follow the same rules. Whenever you are making any major purchase, make sure you are shopping around and comparing prices to get the best deals. There is no point in buying something expensive and then bragging about it, when you can buy the same thing at a lower price. A lot of so-called rich people have the tendency to show off the fact that they don't buy things when they're on sale or use discounts because they find them "cheap." But guess what, nobody (apart from your bank account) cares if you got something during a sale. Rich people like to put up a show that they have a lot of money, while wealthy people take steps to protect the money that they have earned. This includes comparing prices and looking for ways to save money in every transaction they make.

Here's a Piece of Advice...

Understanding your emotions about money and taking steps to improve them is no easy task. It takes courage and perseverance. You are bound to face a number of challenges and face your fears while doing so, but you've got to remember that once you fix your relationship with money, financial planning, and management will become easier for life.

Don't complicate the journey by overthinking but try to divert that energy into evaluating all possible scenarios and preparing yourself for them. Financial planning will help you find answers and deal with the worst-case situations. Here's how simple it will look once you get the hang of managing your goals.

Question: What if I am in an accident and have to be on complete bed rest for six weeks?

Answer: That's not a problem, you have an emergency fund that'll help you cover your daily expenses during this time.

Question: What if I am unable to afford the monthly repayments for all my loans?

Answer: That's not a problem, you already know about credit settlement. You can get in touch with your creditors to negotiate favorable terms and get your debt settled.

So, you see where we are going with this, right? You've got to get into the attitude of "that's not a problem" while dealing with your finances because it will give you confidence and the ability to face any kind of problem efficiently.

Importance of Financial Education

It goes without saying that financial education is one of the most essential aspects of building a positive money mindset and creating wealth. Ignorance is probably the biggest issue that stops people from living up to their full potential when it can be fixed so easily. One of the best things about living in the

21st century is that information is abundantly available, and you can learn things quickly.

Even though it is such an essential skill, financial literacy is still not widely taught in schools or even colleges. So, it is your duty to educate yourself and stay updated regarding all the changes that take place in this sector. It will help you feel more confident about money and make well-informed decisions. No matter how young (or old) you are, it is never a bad time to start learning about your finances. And once you begin, you have to keep at it all your life because it is the only way to make sure you are doing justice to the money you are earning.

Practicing Gratitude and Abundance

Despite all the education and rationalizing, you might sometimes find yourself in situations where nothing seems to work. You can have a bad day at school or work, and all your plans can seem wrecked. If you're ever having such a moment when everything feels out of control, sit down and take a deep breath. Have a glass of water even if you are not thirsty. Then look around the room and try to find a few of your favorite things. It can be an old toy, your best pair of shoes, or anything that you particularly love. Take a moment to appreciate it and think of all the other things that you can be grateful for. Even when it seems everything is terrible, you will find that life has bestowed many blessings on you. If you can't think of anything, be grateful that you have a roof over your head, food and water to sustain yourself, and clothes to protect you from heat and cold. I know it sounds like a cliche, but expressing gratitude toward the most basic things will help you feel grounded and escape the spiral of negative thoughts. Gratitude has a calming effect on your mind and body and allows you to think rationally. It also lets you see and appreciate everything that you have instead of only focusing on what you don't. You can also try affirmations to encourage yourself to feel more grateful.

Once you're feeling slightly better and seem to be escaping the spiral, have a piece of chocolate (or any food that lifts your mood) and write about all the things you feel grateful for. You can also look up journal prompts that let you say thanks to yourself and feel grounded. A money mindset is built through a combination of a lot of things. Just like you have to budget and set financial goals, you'll also have to ensure that you are not undoing your progress during moments of stress.

Having a positive money mindset is an essential money skill that you'll need to master because it will help you shift your perspective and become more comfortable with your finances. Talking about money and dealing with it can seem intimidating for a lot of us, especially if there has been a lot of stigma regarding financial discussions at home. Fixing your money mindset is the first step you can take to delve deeper into the process of becoming a true money master. Once you don't feel awkward talking about money anymore, you'll be able to approach financial management with a lot more confidence.

Chapter 4:

Taming Financial Management

If we command our wealth, we shall be rich and free. If our wealth commands us, we are poor indeed. –Edmund Burke

All through my childhood, I used to spend Thanksgiving at my Aunt Stella's place in Nantucket. It was a packed gathering, where family members from different parts of the country would come for a two-day party. My aunt loved hosting us, and she would remember to take care of everything every year, without fail. Her place certainly wasn't large enough to accommodate 20 people, but everyone always had comfortable places to sleep, along with clean linens. Although we tried to help, she did most of the cooking herself and even managed to keep the house clean during those couple of days. It was always magical, and I was amazed by how well she took care of everything. Aunt Stella stopped hosting Thanksgiving quite a few years back because her health had declined, but I met her recently at my cousin's wedding. During all those years of spending Thanksgiving at her place, I never got to speak with her personally, but I finally had my chance and asked her how she pulled the gathering off so efficiently every year. "Management! That's the secret. You've got to know the whole situation, evaluate what might go wrong, and prepare for all sorts of contingencies!"

Even though this was an old lady sharing her wisdom about how she organized a big party, I feel Aunt Stella's suggestions are extremely valid in the discussion about our finances. Planning and proper management are of pivotal importance when you're trying to achieve financial freedom. The future is uncertain, but you can definitely take steps to ensure you are protected and ready to deal with any kind of contingencies that may come your way. That is why in this chapter, we will be talking about financial planning in detail and covering different aspects of financial management so you feel confident to step up and manage your money more efficiently.

Why Financial Literacy Is Important

Before we jump into the discussions about financial management, let's first talk about the state of financial literacy and why it is important in this context. According to research conducted by GW University, 69% of millennials awarded themselves high grades in regard to financial knowledge when in reality, researchers found that only 23% showed basic financial literacy and 7% exhibited expert financial knowledge (*The importance of financial literacy*, 2019). A lack of financial literacy is definitely a huge problem, but what is more concerning is that a lot of young people think that they have a good grasp on their finances and can make decisions accordingly.

To understand where you stand, you need to evaluate your knowledge and start from the very basics. Financial literacy is an essential life skill because if you're unable to manage your money properly, you will end up ruining all the hard work you're putting in. What is the point of hustling all the time and earning money, if you cannot live your life peacefully?

It starts with basic things, like being able to read a bank statement, and spreads out to more complex issues, like understanding financial statements and evaluating your exact monetary position. When you take steps to educate yourself, you'll feel more confident about where you stand.

Financial illiteracy gives rise to a wide range of misconceptions and myths surrounding money, which, in turn, builds a negative attitude. We talked a lot about mindset in the previous chapter, but let's bring financial education into the discussion now. When you learn to manage your finances, you'll automatically feel better while dealing with your bills. My high school history teacher often used to say, when you've got to do something, better try to enjoy it because otherwise, it gets even more difficult. Of course, he said this in the context of our history lessons, but I guess it's true for your financial journey too! Money is something that you'll have to deal with all your life, so why not educate yourself and enjoy it? Education will broaden your horizons, and you'll soon be able to view financial management as something more than just another chore.

Getting Started With Financial Management

Financial management is a very broad concept that is used by all kinds of entities in the world. The basics are mostly the same, irrespective of whether it is a company or a person. The main objective is to ensure comprehensive attention toward all the important elements of financial management so that the person or the entity has all their bases covered. Since we're talking about personal financial management in this section, here are the essential things that fall under it:

- **Budgeting:** The first and most important element of any financial management plan is a budget or the process of budgeting. This is the part where you would actually become aware of how much money you are bringing in and where you will be spending it. Budgeting helps you create estimates and provide insights into how much you should be spending under each category. The entire process is the foundational pillar of financial management, and it is crucial for you to understand it completely. Based on your requirements, you need to create a budget and allocate amounts for your routine expenses, savings, and investments. Basically, a budget is the primary plan of action that will help you make informed financial decisions.

- **Investing:** Financial management is heavily concerned with how much money you will be investing for your future and through which channels. Once you make a budget and set aside money for savings, you need to start diverting a part of it toward investments. This is not something you have to do from the first month itself, but the sooner you start, the greater returns you'll be able to reap over time. Simply saving will not be able to help you maintain the value of money, and you have to invest a part of it to beat inflation. Investing is essential to secure your financial future. Don't worry if it sounds too intimidating, we will be talking about these concepts in detail in Chapter 6.

- **Borrowing:** How much debt you've undertaken and how you plan to manage it is an essential part of financial management. Debts are important for buying high-value assets like houses or cars, but you can avoid taking unnecessary loans for your day-to-day expenses. Having a financial management plan will help you categorize your debts and evaluate repayment strategies. Since the process begins with creating a budget, it will also provide insight into how much debt you can actually afford and if you're taking on too much. We've already spoken about debts in the previous chapter, but the reason why we mention it once again is to remind you that debts are also included in your financial management plans.

- **Taxation:** Once you start making money and qualify for paying taxes, you'll have to consider its impact on your total income and how you can account for it. Understanding taxes and how much you owe is very important to avoid penalties and investigations. When you're just getting started, you might feel a bit overwhelmed, which is why it is highly recommended that you get in touch with a tax professional. They will help you calculate your taxes correctly and clarify any doubts that you might have during the process.

Understanding Financial Statements

Even though financial statements are inherently linked to business operations, they are important for personal financial management, too, because they help you categorize and understand everything you own and how you should deal with it. Suppose you decide to become an entrepreneur and launch a startup. Then as the founder, you cannot possibly expect your accountant to explain financial statements to you every time. Or, if you want to take out a mortgage and the lender asks for some detailed statements to get deeper insights into your financials, would it be wise to depend entirely on your consultant? You don't have to start preparing detailed financial statements right from the time you start your journey, but you should know about these documents and how to read them.

Usually, there are three basic financial statements that most people (or even businesses) create:

- statement of profit and loss

- balance sheet

- cash flow statement

Corporations and other large entities often prepare other statements that include financial ratios and comparisons. But most of these other documents are created from figures obtained from any of the above-mentioned basic statements. Let us understand what they contain and how you can use them in your personal financial management plan.

Statement of Profit and Loss

A statement of profit and loss is exactly what the name suggests; it is a statement that tells you whether a particular business has made a profit or loss during the specified period. This is the financial document that lists the revenues and the expenses and calculates whether there is a profit or loss. If the income is more than the total expenses combined, then there is profit, and there is a loss if the expenses are more than the income. From a personal financial management perspective, a statement of profit and loss can be helpful in identifying if your current income is sufficient to meet the expenses. This might seem a bit similar to a budget, but there's a difference because budgets also contain estimates and comparisons with the actual amount incurred.

Balance Sheet

A balance sheet is a statement that provides a list of an entity's assets and liabilities as of a certain date. The difference between assets and liabilities is depicted as equity for a business. A personal balance sheet has the same elements as its business counterpart.

While understanding the functionalities of a balance sheet, it is also very important to be aware of its elements. Assets are those items that you own and have the capacity to be converted into cash. For instance, a house in your name, a car, and cash in your bank account are assets. Liabilities are those items that are obligations like debts or any other dues.

The main purpose of a balance sheet is to represent the actual financial position of the entity or person on that date and provide insight into everything they own and owe. It also helps in strategic decision-making and is often used as a reference document by banks and other financial institutions when you're trying to get a loan. A balance sheet should always "balance," which means the total of the assets side must match that of the liabilities side.

A balance sheet is also crucial for an entity as it helps calculate its net worth, which is represented as the difference between assets and liabilities. The objective of any company or person is to have a positive net worth, which means the assets should exceed the liabilities. This is an indication of good financial health and creditworthiness.

Cash Flow Statement

A cash flow statement is one of the most significant financial statements that is useful for both companies and individuals. Just as the name suggests, a cash flow statement shows the movement of cash and cash equivalent coming in and going out during a particular period. It starts with the opening cash balance and then accounts for all the inflows and outflows to arrive at the final closing balance. A cash flow statement uses figures from both an income statement and a balance sheet, which makes it comprehensive and one of the most versatile financial documents. It can hold great significance in personal financial management because it gives insight into all the sources of inflows and then clearly shows where all the money is being spent.

Usually, businesses use all three statements together to evaluate the overall financial situation. When you are just starting your financial management journey, it might feel daunting to prepare so many statements, but if you manage to do so, you'll be able to get a holistic view of your situation. It'll also help you understand the areas for improvement, and you can decide upon an action plan accordingly.

Even though there is a standard framework of financial management, it will look different according to a person's individual needs. For instance, if you're just a student who is still living with your parents, you probably won't be worried a lot about debts or taxes. However, you still need to educate yourself about these elements because you'll be needing the information sooner or later. The objective of having a financial management plan is to be aware of everything that is covered under the umbrella of "personal finance" and prepare yourself for things that might emerge in the course of time.

Protecting Your Finances

One of the biggest and most important elements of financial management is taking steps to protect everything that you are building. Over the course of your journey, you'll be following plans to achieve your financial goals, but how can you make sure you're staying on track at all times? No matter what you do, you've got to ensure that you're not undoing all the progress you've made. Life isn't predictable, and unexpected things can completely deviate you from your financial management goals. Here are a few important tips to follow to make sure you're protecting your finances at all costs:

- **Build an emergency fund:** You know it already, but we cannot emphasize its importance enough. Building an emergency fund can solve an array of problems, and you can live life without the fear of unexpected events wrecking your financial progress. No matter what your other goals are, building an emergency fund that covers at least three to six months of your living expenses should be one of your top priorities right from the time you start the process of financial management.

- **Getting adequate insurance:** As young adults, we often tend to ignore the fact that anything can happen to us. I'm definitely not saying that you'll have to feel anxious about bad stuff happening to you, but you should ensure that you are prepared for them. The mental turmoil of any mishap is huge, and there is usually no way to prepare yourself for that. In times of distress, the best thing you can do is make financial arrangements and have enough money for comfortable sustenance. An emergency fund is one step in that direction, but for greater and more comprehensive coverage, you'd need to take out insurance. Basic health insurance is always the first thing to consider (if your employer doesn't provide it) because healthcare is expensive. Depending on where you are located, you could potentially be spending thousands of dollars for even very simple procedures. Apart from health, you should also consider getting life insurance, especially if you are a single earner in your family. Life insurance will ensure that your family members are taken care of if something happens to you unexpectedly. Protecting your assets is also an important consideration, and that is why you need to get renters'/homeowners' insurance too.

- **Prepare for natural disasters:** The sudden outbreak of the COVID-19 pandemic is a clear indication that despite technological advancements, we have very little control over such events. The same goes for natural disasters like hurricanes, tornadoes, and floods, which is why you have to be financially prepared for them. Think of all the ways your regular life can change when something like this happens—your house may get damaged, you might need to buy new furniture, and if there is widespread destruction, you might need to take some time off from work for a few days. Make sure you have the money to afford all the changes you'll have to make.

- **Have a second budget:** By now, you know that your budget is the most important financial management tool, and you have to follow it rigorously. Apart from the budget that you'll be using every month, create a backup budget where you cut back on a lot of frills and have only the basics. Make this second budget right from the beginning so that you have a clear mind regarding what to keep. When you're in a financial crunch or a situation where you have to cut back immediately, then you can quickly refer to the second budget and start following it. Creating a budget when you're already under pressure and facing an emergency situation can be difficult and overwhelming. There is a high chance of making mistakes and messing it up further because you might not be in a position to think straight. Having a backup budget can seem like an insignificant thing, but it can save you in your most difficult times.

Investing for Your Future and Managing Risk

There is no single way to completely protect your finances. Instead, you'll have to adopt a bunch of strategies and combine them for the best results. Just like you need to take out insurance, build an emergency fund, and have a second budget, you also have to start investing in your future to create a sustainable financial management plan. You can create a budget and savings plan in your late teens or early twenties, but unless you are making enough money in the future, you won't be able to follow through with your plans, and the entire process will fall apart.

When we say, "investing for the future," there are two aspects to that statement.

- First, you have to create a financial investment plan for yourself. As soon as you're comfortable with savings, start diverting a part of it toward investments. As a young adult, you can invest in pretty much anything you want because you have all the time in the world to recover from any mistakes that you might make. But it is still safer to start with the traditional forms of investment like stocks, bonds, mutual funds, and exchange-traded funds. The trick here is to start as early as you can so that you can reap the maximum benefits of compounding and generate great returns. When you create a profitable investment stream, you'll be able to achieve all your financial goals. The point here is to create a budget and stick to it all your life. Of course, you should be modifying the budget according to changing needs and priorities. Long-term investments can help you tremendously as you grow older because you'll always have funds to fall back on in case something doesn't work out.

- The second investment that you'll be making is in yourself. This includes taking care of your physical and mental health and planning your education. No matter what happens, remember that you are the most important part of this entire process. So, you've got to stay healthy and educate yourself so you can maintain your income stream. Investing in education can look different for everyone. A lot of people do not believe in the traditional college education but opt for skill development instead, which is perfectly fine. But if you can afford it, a bachelor's degree might be worth it because a lot of companies only hire college graduates. Moreover, if you're interested in further pursuing education, a college degree will open doors for graduate school and even a PhD. It is also important to note here that taking out a loan for your education is also worth it because a fancy degree definitely increases your chances of securing a better job.

Overcoming Problems

When you're planning and investing for the future, you'll most likely face a lot of strange situations. Life rarely goes according to our plans because there are so many changes happening all at once. Whenever something unexpected happens, our priorities shift, and financial management takes a backseat. As you grow older, you'll realize that problems are more common than you can imagine, but you can't let everything bother you. Of course, you're allowed to feel upset when something bad happens, but the best course of action is to evaluate the situation and be prepared to face it because denial isn't going to get you anywhere. Although every person has their unique set of issues, here are some common problems (and their solutions) many young adults tend to face as they grow up and navigate the complexities of financial management.

- **Sudden lifestyle change after moving out:** Moving out of your parent's house can be an exciting prospect. You're going to college or getting a new job, living on your own, and making a new life for yourself. Despite all the thrill, many young adults get an unpleasant surprise when they find out that living on their own isn't as easy as it seems. When you have stayed with your parents for all your life, you get used to a certain type of lifestyle. For instance, your laundry is done regularly, you get good meals twice a day along with breakfast every morning, and usually, you don't have to worry when essential things like toilet paper or bread are gone. But when you start living alone, all of this is going to be on you. Even if you are a responsible person, it is very easy to get overwhelmed by the amount of work you'll suddenly have. As a result, you might lash out and start behaving irresponsibly, which in turn can affect your finances. You can be tempted to overspend or buy things impulsively to release stress. All of these are natural, and you should not be blaming yourself if that happens. Instead, try to address the issue by being prepared for it. Before you leave home, sit with your parents and make a list of all the things you'll need to remember when you're living alone. You might be missing certain things, but it's still better than being completely unprepared. If your dorm room or apartment doesn't seem good enough, remember that your parents worked hard to get where they are now. They probably didn't start with the house you live in now, so you also have to be patient with yourself and manage your expectations so that you can avoid frustration.

- **Sudden unemployment or illness:** I know nobody likes to think about it, but suffering a job loss is actually more common than you can imagine. In the present economic scenario, companies often tend to conduct mass layoffs to cut costs, and people lose their jobs despite doing their very best. If something like that happens to you, make sure you're prepared to take care of yourself financially until you get the next gig. Start networking immediately and look for suitable opportunities according to your skills and qualifications. Even though this is not an easy thing to deal with, having a financial backup in the form of emergency funds can be very helpful. The same logic applies to a sudden illness or accident too. When you're physically sick, you won't be able to work like you did before, and you'll need time to get back on your feet. Make sure you have insurance to pay for the treatment and money to sustain yourself during this time.

- **Surprises that may or may not be pleasant:** Life is filled with surprises, and while some of them are very pleasant, others might not. For instance, you can suddenly meet the love of your life and decide to get married even when you had no plans of doing so. Then you have your first child, and you feel really happy with your spouse and kid. Even if you love your partner and are thrilled to be a parent, the sudden surprise of additional expenses might be too much to handle. You're looking at doctor's appointments, multiple loads of laundry, and a lot of diapers. All of these things can be exhausting and expensive, which is why you need to create separate funds for these events. Even if you don't have plans to have kids or get married, set aside funds so that you can deal with these new changes with a smile on your face.

You will probably face different kinds of problems as you grow older. Money might not be able to solve all those problems, but it can definitely make things smoother. Going through life with your loved ones becomes easier when you know you're financially prepared.

Human beings are social creatures. No matter how much you try to do things alone, you need other people to survive and live life harmoniously. Personal financial management is often considered to be something that people need to do alone because it's their money and their decision at the end of the day. But to be really successful and create wealth, mastering your finances alone won't be enough. You have to manage the way you work and interact with people around you because they influence your decisions too. That is why in the next chapter, we will focus on building and maintaining good relationships so that they can contribute to your healthy financial future.

Chapter 5:

Quality Relationships

The meeting of two personalities is like the contact of two chemical substances: if there is any reaction, both are transformed. —Carl Gustav Jung

In my freshman year of college, my roommate, Dean, was a quarterback on the football team. He also played tennis and was a great swimmer. Naturally, he was quite the fitness enthusiast who would wake up at the crack of dawn to go for runs. I kept my distance from him during the first few days, but eventually, he would pull me out of my bed every morning and make me accompany him. At that time, I was embracing the college experience, and the whole fitness vibe was quite refreshing. Even before they became trendy, I was having smoothies for breakfast and salads for dinner. To be completely honest with you, I was never that person who would go for runs or eat salads. My go-to meal was a cheeseburger, but gradually, I started enjoying eating healthy. Dean and I were roommates for two years until he graduated. In my senior year, I got a new roommate, Matthew, who was a night owl and survived on chips. Remembering Dean and how instrumental his role was in making me a fitness enthusiast, I started making breakfast for Matthew and sharing my fruit bowls with him. I wouldn't say I converted him, but I did find him snacking on apples instead of Funyuns after a few months.

Our friends, families, and even acquaintances have the beautiful ability to touch our lives in different ways. It can be good habits like waking up early, taking care of our health, or managing our finances in a certain way. Yes, you read that right! Your relationships can affect your financial management endeavors very heavily, and they can be both positive and negative. The actions can be very subtle, but the impacts are deep, which is why in this chapter, we will be looking at how our relationships can shape our financial planning process and how we can make the best of it.

Are Your Relationships Hurting Your Finances?

You might not be aware of it, but many of your relationships could actually be hurting your financial journey. Relationships are very delicate, and it can often become difficult to identify the red flags, especially when we are very close to the person concerned. That is why before talking about the financial aspects, let us delve deeper into how you can evaluate your relationships.

Whenever people talk about "relationships," somehow, the focus automatically goes toward our romantic associations. Here we are talking about *all* our relationships, not just the romantic ones.

Signs of Dysfunctional Family Relationships

Although nobody likes to talk about it (or even admit it), there can be a lot of dysfunction in our family relationships which can take a toll on your overall mental health and financial planning process. Here are some common pointers that might indicate dysfunctional family relationships:

- Family members might not encourage open communication among themselves. In fact, if someone is going through a personal struggle, they are asked to keep it to themselves instead of sharing it with others.

- Not taking responsibility for wrongdoings. Even if a family member has done something wrong, they shy away from taking any responsibility or might even shift the blame to someone (or something) else.

- Family members are always trying to put up a show in front of outsiders. This includes deceptive behavior and becoming a different person when others are around.

- Older family members try to intimidate the children or other younger members because they are "kids" or "don't have enough experience in life." They might also demean members who do not make any money or less than how much they make.

Remember, the point of this discussion isn't to point fingers at your family or how they behave but to help you identify problematic behaviors and take action accordingly. If a member of your family has any of the above traits, they might impact your outlook on life and finances negatively. The focus here should be on you and improving your financial approach. Who knows, your first step toward building healthier relationships might motivate your entire family to do so as well.

Dysfunctional Romantic Relationships

Our romantic relationships are not that different from our family ties which is why the elements of dysfunction are also quite similar to the ones we talked about above. If your partner doesn't communicate with you properly or makes you feel bad about your choices (even though there's nothing wrong with them), there are probably some problems in the relationship that go beyond the regular fights that every couple has. A lot of dysfunctional couples don't even realize that their or their partner's behavior isn't normal unless someone expressly points it out. For instance, arguments for couples in unhealthy relationships often tend to look like a war where one or both of them spiral out of control and bring up things that have no connection to the topic they are currently arguing about.

Once again, we're not analyzing the problems in relationships just for the sake of it but to make you aware of them and how they might be impacting your financial journey.

How Problematic Relationships Affect Your Finances

Problematic relationships can create numerous issues in our lives. Even though it is not that apparent, they have a very negative impact on our financial management journey too. Many people have grown up in families where they have seen one of their parents dominate the household because they are the main breadwinner. These people are more likely to associate money with power and exhibit the same kind of behavior in their own families. This not only encourages a negative money mindset but also creates an adverse impact on the other family members, especially the children. As a child, if you've seen your parents tell you things like, "You are not allowed to have an opinion on this matter because you're not a contributing member of the family," there is a high chance you'll continue to feel the same way in your life. Your whole sense of worth could become attached to how much money you're making, and if you're not making enough, you'll declare yourself a failure.

A lot of parents also have the tendency to not discuss money matters in front of their kids. They probably want to protect the children, but it does more harm than good. People who grow up with the belief that talking about money isn't "nice" feel uncomfortable around their finances. Sooner or later, they have to deal with money, and when that time comes, they have no clue about how to handle things. I've seen many adults who are highly educated and established in their fields struggle with simple things like banking and maintaining a steady savings rate. It's not their fault, money isn't something that is taught in school unless you're studying finance. If parents also don't discuss financial matters with their kids, they can grow up to be financially illiterate adults.

There are similar instances in romantic relationships too. If you don't talk to your partner about money, there is no way for them to understand how you feel about it. Suppose they come from a different financial background than you and are used to overspending on almost all occasions. Just to put up the show and pretend you're the same, you can end up going over your budget and messing up your whole spending plan. Not being honest in romantic relationships about money is a very common occurrence, and if you're doing that, then it might be time to stop. Lack of communication about finances can lead to other more severe issues like lying about money and potentially wreaking all your progress.

If your partner doesn't have a clear idea about your financial goals, then they will never be on the same page as you. When you're living with someone, and they don't share your financial mindset, it can be catastrophic for your finances.

Building Healthy Relationships With Your Peers

It might seem like you've entered a mental health seminar, but building healthy relationships is very important for your overall functioning. You'll become a more well-rounded person who doesn't hesitate to put their needs in front of others. From the previous section, you've already seen that there's a deep connection between your relationships and how you handle your finances. Apart from your family and romantic relationships, your peer group also plays a major role in your attitude toward money and how you're managing it. If you're moving out of your parents' house for higher education, you'll be staying with your college buddies for the maximum time. That is why choosing the correct peer group almost becomes as important as choosing a suitable romantic partner. Since you'll be spending the most time with your friends, there is a high chance that their behavior and approach toward life are going to influence you too. Don't think you're too gullible if you get easily swayed, it is only normal and is very common human behavior. Think about my lifestyle change while I was living with Dean during my college years. Even if I wasn't initially enjoying it very much, I would get up and go for runs with him. That was a positive experience and shows the huge role your peer group can play in your life.

Importance of Quality Friendships to Develop Personal Finances

Healthy relationships can be instrumental in improving your overall functioning and have a great impact on your financial journey. We often underestimate the role of our friends in our day-to-day lives, but they actually play a very important role in the choices we make and the way we approach things. As young adults navigating all the complexities of life, it is very easy to feel burdened or overwhelmed with so much responsibility. That is when we turn to our friends for moral support and comfort. When you're staying with your parents, they provide you with a certain kind of comfort and protection. You have a house to live in, and usually, they will take care of your basic needs. If you're not working during your high school days, your parents will either provide you with an allowance or give you money when you need something. But it all changes once you move out.

Friends start playing a major role in our daily lives. Despite phones and video chats, you'll realize that life becomes very different when your parents are not around. The independence associated with living alone is two-fold—while there's a fun part where you get to do what you want, there's also additional responsibility to ensure you're taking care of yourself. In such cases, we often turn to our friends for support and advice. Think about it, there's a test in two days, and your department seniors have thrown a huge party that evening. It feels stupid to miss it because you know it's going to be awesome, but you also feel guilty for not studying for the test. In this situation, it is unlikely that you'll call up your parents and ask for their suggestions. You'll probably end up talking to your roommate or friends and asking them if they're going too.

The same goes with regular mundane decisions too. Suppose you need to buy a new laptop, and you know a couple of your friends bought theirs a few days ago. So, you'll obviously ask them for their opinion and might even end up buying the one they suggest because their word means something to you. Even if their suggestion exceeds your budget, you might be tempted to buy it since you trust their opinion and have seen them work on their new laptop. Friends have the ability to influence us very subtly, which can, in turn, have an effect on our finances.

How Peer Groups Impact Your Finances and What You Can Do About It

When you're young, friendship has a lot to do with being included. You want to get invited to hangouts, share secrets, and become a member of the group. If your friends ask you to go shopping with them, you'll go because that's what friends do. Even if you didn't have any plans (or money) to shop for unnecessary things, you'll still buy some stuff to give them company. That is where it all starts. Once you begin compromising your budgets and financial plans to fit in with your friends, you are at the risk of undoing all the progress you've made.

If you feel that your friends might be distracting you from your financial journey, here are a few things you can do:

- Be honest about your situation. When you don't have enough money to spend on hangouts, shopping, or parties, have an open line of communication and let them know you won't be able to make it. Being able to say no can save you from a lot of trouble later on.

- Share your financial priorities with your closest friends. Instead of canceling expensive plans, let them know why you can't spend money on those things. If you let your friends know that you are saving up for a car or have a ton of student debt, they are more likely to be understanding and supportive.

- Set some ground rules for yourself. Remember the time when you first started going out with friends and your parents had a curfew for you? Implement something similar to protect your financial plans. It all starts with that one bad decision, and before everything blows up and it's too late to undo all the damage, set some rules.

- Always remember your financial goals, especially when you are very tempted to go out and spend money with your friends. Make sure your budget allows you to have some fun because life can get really monotonous if you're not indulging yourself.

I hate to be the bearer of bad news, but if your friends do not understand your financial situation, then you need to choose better friends. They should not be making you feel bad about skipping events because of money problems. You have a very distinct set of priorities, and you need to stay true to them. Real friends will always understand your situation and support you as much as they can.

Family Relationships and Finance

By now, we've established that our family values play a major role in the way we deal with money. Now let's talk about how we can initiate the conversation and talk to our family members regarding financial issues. Here are a few tips that you can follow:

- If your family members don't usually include you in any of their financial discussions, then you'll need to throw the topic at them carefully. Talk to one of your parents first and let them know that you have been reading up about saving money and you were wondering if they could provide you with some insight. Get your parents talking about it and ask them when a good time would be to have an open discussion about it. If you have a sibling, make sure to include them, too, even if they are younger. You will never be able to create a healthy financial attitude in your home if everyone doesn't participate in the discussion.

- Ask your parents about things that they already know about. For instance, you can ask them how taxes work and the process they follow every year to get their taxes filed. If they have a financial consultant, you can request them to let you tag along the next time they have an appointment. You have to make an effort to communicate that you are genuinely interested in learning about finances, and you feel that your parents can help you in the best possible ways. This could also be a good chance to find out how aware they are. There's a possibility that both of you might learn things together.

- Share your personal financial goals with your parents and let them know that you've started making a budget. Most parents will be extremely happy to discover that their kids are becoming responsible about money. Your parents might have created savings or kept aside funds for your education. Make sure you're aware of the whole financial situation because you deserve to know.

- If you're already married and have kids, you should initiate an open conversation about money. Kids need to learn that money is just another topic, and it is okay to talk about it. As a child, you might not have received proper financial education from your parents, but you can always break that cycle by making your kids financially literate. Discuss the topic with your partner to make an action plan and ensure that the two of you are on the same page. Encourage your kids to ask questions and be very patient with them as they try to understand the different financial concepts.

I do understand that not all of our family members are equally flexible when it comes to financial discussions, and that is okay. You probably won't be able to change their entire belief system overnight, but the point is to make them feel you're ready to learn about finances and would love to include them in the discussion.

Romantic Relationships and Finance

Money isn't something that people like to talk about with their romantic partners because they feel like it spoils the mystery of the relationship. But honestly, you don't want your relationship to get *that* mysterious. Not sharing your monetary insights can get quite catastrophic, especially if you are living with that person. There will be a constant state of hide and seek at home where you'll have to pretend to be someone you're not. To avoid that, you'll have to identify the potential issues and act accordingly. Here are some of the most common problems that young couples face while dealing with money:

- **Not having "the talk":** You've started living with your partner for a while now, but it still seems like an extension of the first date. Both of you are splitting the check every time you eat out, and there are no clear ground rules about how the household expenses are being shared.

- **Not knowing each other's financial backgrounds:** A lot of couples tend to avoid talking about their financial background because they feel uncomfortable and are scared that their partner might judge them. As a result, both of them are completely unaware of how they were brought up and what their financial goals are.

- **Keeping secrets:** Even after living together for years, many couples keep monetary secrets from their partners. This can take the form of money hidden in secret places or having a bank account that their partner doesn't know about.

- **Only one person managing the finances:** This is a very common thing where one of the partners takes all financial responsibilities and makes decisions while the other person has no clue about what's going on.

While these problems might not seem like a big deal at first, they can create a lot of problems later on. As a couple, you and your partner need to discuss money matters even if it feels uncomfortable. Once you have crossed that initial barrier, you'll feel like a weight being lifted off your shoulders. If you're the one taking all the responsibility, talk to them about sharing it and how you'd like to do that. Including your partner in financial discussions is the best decision you will ever make. Think about it, you're building a life together, and finances play a huge role in how you live your life. If you're not talking about money, are you really being honest in your relationship?

Shared financial goals are extremely healthy and improve the bond between you and your partner. If you are planning to buy a house, savings from two sources will make the process faster. Talk about your goals and plans and see if they align with that of your partner. Don't expect everything to fit perfectly because you're two different people, but unless you have the talk, there's no way to know. You might find out that you have more in common with your partner than you thought, and a lot of your financial goals actually match.

You spend the most time with the people who are closest to you. That is why they have a lot of influence over your financial attitude and spending behavior. If you're not being careful about how you spend your money alone or with people you love, you might find yourself being unable to save or invest money. Savings and investments are two of the most essential elements of your journey toward achieving financial freedom. That is why in the next chapter, we will be talking about these concepts in detail and helping you understand the suitable options for you according to your priorities.

Chapter 6:

Save and Invest

To acquire money requires valor, to keep money requires prudence, and to spend money well is an art. –Berthold Auerbach

A few years ago, my doctor told me that I needed to lose some weight. My fitness enthusiast days from college were behind me, and work pressure had made me quite unhealthy. It wasn't anything major, but I wanted to make sure that I was taking care of my body, which is why I immediately started following a strict diet and an exercise regimen. I followed this for two months, and when I went back to the doctor again for another checkup, he said my weight was now at the correct levels. Of course, I was overjoyed, so I treated myself to a fancy Starbucks coffee on my way home. I had worked hard and lost weight, so I thought I deserved it. But it quickly started going downhill from there because even though losing weight once was easy, maintaining it was very hard. I needed a consistent plan of action to make sure I wasn't ruining my progress.

Our financial journey is actually more similar to this story than we'd like to admit. Simply earning money isn't enough because you won't be able to sustain it unless you're taking steps to protect it. Saving and investing money is essential to future-proof your financial plans. That is why in this chapter, we'll walk you through the importance of saving and investing and help you identify the best ways to do so based on your priorities.

Understanding Savings and Practicing It

I'm sure that you've heard people say it a million times that saving money is extremely important. But let's talk about the "why" behind that statement.

When you're just starting your financial management journey, you'll be coming across different kinds of rules and principles, and all of them direct you toward a single objective: You need to have enough money to afford the things you need and want and ensure that your future is protected. To ensure you are doing all of that smoothly, you have to start saving money right from the beginning.

As a young adult who is still living with parents or has just started earning, saving might seem a bit impractical. When you're not making enough money, saving money seems absurd, right? But that's not how it works. Even if your income isn't sufficient, you can start your savings journey. The key here is to take baby steps.

Your income level might be low at the moment, but it will increase over time. But if you wait till then to start your savings journey, it might just be too late. Don't get me wrong, I'm not saying you can't start saving at an older age, but it's easier to build a habit when you're young and have fewer priorities. Here are a few important reasons why saving is so important in your financial journey:

- Money issues are the biggest contributors to a large number of physical and mental health problems. When you have a lot of financial responsibility and no certainty regarding how you'll be repaying it in time, it is very obvious to feel stressed out. We do not give enough importance to maintaining peace of mind in our lives until we face a financial crisis. Saving money is important to avoid all these problems and lead a peaceful life. Even if there are any inconsistencies with your regular source of income, the money you have saved will help you in meeting your financial obligations.

- When you have a lot of money saved, you get the luxury of making different kinds of choices. Life doesn't always go according to plan, and you might need to make significant changes depending on the present situation. Let's talk about my cousin Isobelle and how saving money helped her when she decided to make a major change in her life. Isobelle studied engineering and took the first job offer she got after graduating from college. Unfortunately, she lost her job after a couple of years during a round of mass layoffs. Although she was mentally quite devastated by this sudden unemployment, Isobelle had enough money saved up to help sustain herself until she got a new job. She was very particular about her savings goals, and the first thing she did after getting a job was to build an emergency fund. During the two years she was working, she saved aggressively and created multiple funds, which she eventually used after losing her job. While she was looking for new opportunities, she had a lot of free time, which allowed her to rekindle her passion for doodling and designing. She was posting these on her social media frequently, and her designs got noticed by a human resource manager of a budding startup. They reached out to her and asked her if she would like to work at their company as a freelance graphic designer. Isobelle knew the basic tools, but she was no professional, and the company was really keen on working with her. So, she accepted the gig, and even though it did not pay as much as her previous job, it was a start. Soon, Isobelle took a professional graphic designing course online and started getting more clients who would assign specialized projects to her. She completely switched her career trajectory, and it was a change for the better because she now has a thriving freelancer business with over 20 clients. Isobelle could make this career change because she had money saved up, and it would have been impossible if she had to constantly worry about making ends meet during this transitional time.

- Most of us work full-time jobs to earn enough money to sustain ourselves. But where does it end? Do you think it would be feasible for you to keep on working at this pace even when you are in your 50s or 60s? When you reach a certain age, you might want to retire and take a break from the constant hustle. Then again, how will you afford your lifestyle if there isn't enough money? Saving money from a young age can help you retire at a comfortable age with a nest egg. Just because you're not earning anymore doesn't mean your lifestyle and standard of living will drastically change. You'll still expect to do all the things you did before, but without the money coming in, you'll need to make proper financial provisions. You must have seen many happy people who have the time of their life after retirement. They travel the world and try out new things, and all of that is only possible when you save money from a young age.

Tips to Save Money

Now that we've made a case for saving money, let's come to how you can start doing it. In all the previous chapters, we've talked about how dedicating 20% of your income toward savings is recommended. But when your income doesn't seem to be enough to meet all your expenses, saving money can lose its importance. A lot of the time, we feel we don't have money to save when, in reality, we are ignoring some very obvious cues. If you feel the same and are confused about how to start, here are a few time-tested tips that you can follow.

- The first and most important thing to do is to automate your savings. Set up deposits for a specific day of each month so that the money is directly transferred to your savings account. This method might come across as imposing but trust me, it works like a charm. Transferring money to your savings account by yourself seems easy, but it can often get ignored especially when you have a lot going on. Automate the transfer and forget about the fact that you are saving money. Put your savings journey on autopilot mode to get the maximum benefits.

- We often tend to overspend the most on food and groceries. Suppose you've gone grocery shopping with your partner or roommate, and you are walking through the snack aisle. You promised yourself that you won't purchase too many snacks, but the choices leave you overwhelmed, and you decide to pick out six bags of chips instead of two. Even if we have a very tight budget, we tend to lose it at the grocery stores, especially in the snacks and candy aisles. To prevent this, prep before you go shopping. Make a list of all the things you need and put a checkmark next to each one once you've picked them up. Allow yourself some wiggle room and allocate $5–$10 toward additional impulse stuff but make sure you don't exceed that under any circumstances. Also, don't go grocery shopping while you're hungry because you will definitely end up buying extra stuff in anticipation of everything you'll cook.

- I know it sounds cliche, but to encourage yourself to save money, you have to learn to cut back on some of your expenses. Start with reviewing your budget, especially the "wants" category, and how much you are spending on eating out, online shopping, and subscriptions. While there's nothing wrong with indulging yourself, it is also important to know when and what to cut back on to save more money. If that sounds like you're depriving yourself, remember all the financial goals you've set and the things you want to achieve. If you're eating out four times a week, cut that back to two and start creating a schedule for preparing meals in advance. Take a good look at all your subscriptions and remove the ones you haven't used in the past two months. If you have a full-time job or are a student, you are spending eight hours or more every day at work or school, and there's no way you can watch shows and movies on all your streaming services. Cancel the ones you don't use, or consider getting a shared plan with your friends. You might even want to review your gym and other fitness subscriptions too. If you are a student, look for gyms on campus that provide discounts to students.

- Speaking of cutting back expenses, make sure you are restricting online shopping too. It is one of the biggest contributors to credit card debt, and you don't want the dues piling up every month. If you cannot control your urge to order random things online, uninstall a few of the concerned apps. Online shopping can also promote hoarding tendencies. For instance, you can end up buying essential things before you actually need them because there's a "sale" going on. No matter how much of a discount you're getting, you don't need to buy five avocados and four packs of cherries.

- Even though it seems a little old school, exclusively use cash for some of your expenses, especially the ones where you tend to overspend. Using cash eliminates the option of spending extra money on something because you're not giving yourself the chance to do so. Grocery shopping is one common area where we tend to go overboard. Consult your budget and see how much you've estimated for weekly groceries, and then take approximately that amount of cash when you go out. If the bill comes to more than you have, you'll automatically know the things that you need to remove. I started doing this a few years ago, and it has helped me save so much. Both me and my partner love buying random stuff from Target, which is why we decided to carry cash for our weekly visits. The person at our checkout counter informed us that the bill was almost $51 more than what we had, so we started removing stuff from the cart. Turns out, we didn't need the imported parmesan block, the fancy cooking wine, or the truffle-flavored chips. Needless to say, all those things were extra, and we could easily eliminate them to save money.

- If you have a big social circle and there's always a party or someone's birthday coming up, get a bit creative with the gifts. You don't have to get your friends expensive things or show up with a fancy bottle of wine at every party. These gestures might make you popular within the group, but you won't be doing any favors to yourself or your financial journey if you keep spending money on these things. If you like to give nice gifts, opt for handmade stuff or search thrift stores for unique things. It'll have a personal touch, and you won't be burning a hole in your pocket.

Apart from all the tips mentioned above, one of the most important things that you can do to increase savings is to get rid of high-interest debt as soon as you can. Debts like credit cards that carry a very high-interest rate can mess up your savings goal tremendously. If you're making the minimum payment and still using the card to make purchases, the balance will keep on increasing every month, and eventually, you'll find that you are unable to maintain the repayments. Go back to your budget and see how you can manage to repay these debts quickly. We've already talked a lot about debt management and the steps you can take to evaluate your situation. Allocate small amounts of money to the highest-interest debts every month to speed up the repayment process. If you've recently started cutting back your expenses and have some extra cash in your hands that hasn't been allotted to anything specific, use the money toward your debts. Eliminating debt and staying true to your financial priorities will help you tremendously when you're trying to save money.

Cracking the Investment Code

Now that you've gained insight into savings, let's talk about investments. Savings and investments are the two most significant elements of any personal financial management plan. Once you are comfortable with the idea of regularly setting money aside from your income and creating specific funds for achieving your financial goals, you can think about venturing into investments.

Investments are assets that are acquired with the objective of earning income or enjoying the benefits of appreciation over time (Hayes, 2021). This means that when you make an investment, you expect to earn money from it. If you're holding the asset for a long time, you also expect it to increase in value so that if you decide to sell it, you can make a profit. These two features of investments make it different from saving because when you're saving money, you're not expecting to earn anything from it. Sure, savings accounts in banks or other financial institutions provide you with interest for keeping the money there, but the rates are really low, and it can't really be considered as "income." If you want your money to work for you and fetch you actual returns, you need to divert a part of your savings into investments.

Here are a few major reasons why investments are so important for your financial journey:

- Investments are the only way to earn income from the money that you have saved. When you put your money into securities like stocks or bonds, you get to generate returns from them over time.

- As a responsible and rational person, you should think about the long haul. While saving money is important for all your financial goals, investing can help you achieve these goals faster because of the higher rates of return. In the long run, investments can turn out to be extremely profitable because the markets tend to grow, and economies expand over the years.

- Ask your grandparents how much a gallon of milk cost during the 1970s, and you'll understand what inflation is. Over time, the prices of goods and services keep on increasing, which means that the value of the money you hold decreases. Investing is the only way to beat the inflation rates and ensure your money retains its worth.

- When you invest your money, you get the benefit of compounding. This is a process where you earn interest on the amount of money you initially deposit along with the interest earned on it. Let us understand this with the help of an example. Suppose you deposit $1,200 in an investment account that gives you a 10% interest rate. So, at the end of the first year, you'll earn $120 interest, and your final balance would be $1,320 ($1,200 + $120). Assuming you don't invest any extra money, at the end of the second year, you'll earn 10% interest on your accumulated balance of $1,320. This way, the interest income will keep on increasing over time, and you'll be earning phenomenal returns on your investments.

The Concept of Risk in Investing and How to Mitigate It

Despite all the above-mentioned benefits of investing, there is one very significant drawback that causes many people to stay away from it. There is an inherent risk associated with all forms of investments. When you're saving, you're simply setting aside your money in a separate account, but when you're investing, the money is being directed to the markets. That is why when markets fluctuate, the value of your investments change accordingly. During periods of boom, your investments can increase phenomenally, but if markets are down, you are at risk of losing money too.

There is a common saying about investments that the higher the risk, the higher the reward. Historically, high-risk investments have either failed miserably or provided massive returns. But that doesn't mean you'll have to invest in risky securities only. Your investment decisions should be based on your comfort levels. Just because some financial influencer made a big profit with a very risky investment, doesn't mean you have to do so too. In fact, it is recommended that you don't put all your eggs in one basket, which means even if you're comfortable undertaking big risks, you shouldn't put all your money in a single risky security. To mitigate market-related risks, make sure to diversify your investments and select a wide variety of securities. This will ensure that your returns are protected to a great extent, even if the markets are not moving favorably.

Common Types of Investments

Now that you're aware of investments and why they are important, let us look at some of the common investment types that you can choose from:

- **Stocks:** When large corporations need to raise money to expand their business operations or other projects, they issue stocks to the public. They split their capital into a large number of stocks that can be bought by us at a price. These stocks represent ownership in the company and usually come with voting rights. Stocks are great investments because as the company grows, their value will also increase. Many companies also pay dividends to their stockholders, which is a reward for buying the stocks and supporting the company. However, stocks can also be risky because if the company isn't doing well, you won't be making any money from it.

- **Bonds:** When governments and other large corporations require funds, they can choose to issue bonds which are a form of fixed-income securities. As an investor, purchasing a bond is like giving a loan to the concerned company or government. You are entitled to a fixed rate of income every year, which means it is much safer in comparison to stocks. However, the downside is that there is no scope for phenomenal returns.

- **Mutual funds:** If you don't feel confident choosing specific securities to invest in, mutual funds are a great option for you. These securities invest in a pool of funds and allocate the money toward different kinds of stocks, fixed-income securities, and other assets. The advantage of investing in mutual funds is that you don't have to worry about risk management, and the fund will build a diversified portfolio for you.

- **Exchange-traded funds (ETFs):** ETFs are similar to mutual funds, but instead of investing the funds in a large variety of assets, they put the fund money into an entire index. So, the performance of the fund will depend on how the index moves.

- **Individual retirement accounts (IRAs):** These are specialized accounts for encouraging retirement savings. Even if you're not a legal adult yet, your parents can open a custodial IRA for you.

- **401(k):** This is an employer-sponsored retirement savings plan where you can contribute a part of your monthly salary toward this account. Usually, the employer matches your contribution too.

These are usually the most commonly preferred investments among young adults. As you grow older, you might want to explore more options like real estate. If you're interested in a bit of adventure, you can also consider venturing into cryptocurrencies and other digital assets. No matter which investment you choose, make sure you are conducting adequate research about the potential risks and problems. If you still feel confused, get in touch with an investment consultant who can help you figure out the right options according to your priorities.

Striking a Balance

Young adults have often found it very hard to understand the exact ratio between savings and investments. To put it more simply, if you have $100 to set aside, how much should you save, and how much should you invest? Many aggressive investors believe that saving is wasting money because you can never get a good return from putting your money into a savings account. It is almost similar to storing money inside a glass jar where you're simply setting the money aside. While there is a certain degree of logic to this statement, you cannot completely ignore the importance of savings.

Investing money will help you beat inflation and reap phenomenal returns over time, but there's also a certain degree of risk associated with it. The stocks or mutual funds that you put your money in might not perform well due to market fluctuations, and you can even end up incurring a loss on them. Usually, in the long run, investments almost always perform well and provide good returns, but that doesn't mean you'll completely eliminate savings. Try to use the savings channel for your short-term needs. For instance, you should always keep your emergency fund saved because you do not want any fluctuations in that amount. Short-term market changes are very common, which is why you should not put your emergency fund money toward buying stocks or mutual funds. Keep it in a low-interest savings account that offers high liquidity so you can withdraw it anytime you need.

When you're young, you can invest a larger portion of your money to generate high returns. As a rule of thumb, you can dedicate 40% of your additional money toward savings and the remaining 60% toward investments. Based on your risk appetite, you can increase or decrease it too.

Interactive Element: Review Money Savings Apps

Honestly, I feel the most difficult part of saving money is being consistent and sticking to a routine. No matter how old you are, creating a savings habit isn't easy, especially when you are just starting the process. If you're new and struggling to start saving, don't worry because we've got you covered! Thanks to technological advancements, there are a number of savings apps that can help you increase your savings rate through customized strategies that are suitable for you. Here are some of the most popular options:

- **Digit:** If you're a spendthrift and want an app that will help you control your impulses, Digit is the best app for you. It lets you set goals, automate your savings, and even devise strategies to pay down your credit card dues. Digit has a smart algorithm and does not "automatically" deduct money. It evaluates your expenses and stops automatic deposits until it is sure you have enough money to meet basic expenses.

- **Qapital:** This is the perfect app for building up funds through small savings. Qapital allows you to set up savings rules which means the whole process will work according to the norms you set for yourself. It also rounds up your expenses according to the roundup rules you've set and deposits the change to your savings account. This means that if you buy something for $4.75, Qapital will round it up to $5 and deposit $0.25 toward savings.

- **Long Game:** This is a unique savings app that promotes long-term financial planning through a game-like interface. Users can set savings goals and then win prizes once they achieve them. Long Game also provides useful savings tips and customized instructions to its users.

- **Chime:** Chime has been around for almost a decade now and can be a great digital savings platform. You can set up your Chime account and enable direct deposits, which means automating your savings can become much easier.

- **Mint:** This is the only lifetime free app that helps you integrate all your bank accounts and encourage savings. You can create customized budgets and set alerts for bill reminders so that you don't miss anything. Mint is a very useful app and is extremely suitable for beginners.

Saving and investing are two of the major pillars of your journey to becoming a money master. Savings and investments will help you become debt-free faster and truly experience freedom. But that is not the only reason why you should be doing it. When you have enough money saved and invested in different securities, you can choose to live your life the way you wish. Having different choices can be powerful and liberating, and it can lead to further financial success. In the next chapter, we will be discussing the importance of making the right choices and how you can align your priorities to make the best decisions every time.

Chapter 7:

Choices

Every human has four endowments—self-awareness, conscience, independent will, and creative imagination. These give us the ultimate human freedom... The power to choose, to respond, to change. –Stephen Covey

It is 10:30 p.m., and you know it's bedtime, but you decide to relax by scrolling through your phone. You open Facebook first, and then when that gets boring, you open Instagram. You go to the suggestions section and start watching Reels of recipes, dog videos, psychology hacks, relationship advice, and whatnot until you come across a movies page that contains excellent suggestions for new shows and movies. It's about time you watched something new. Even though *Big Bang Theory* is your comfort show, it can get tiring watching it for the fifth time. You choose a new show on Netflix and start watching the first episode. It's only 25 minutes, so you can easily watch one and still go to sleep by 12 a.m. The show turns out to be quite captivating, so you decide to watch the next one too. Surely, another 25 minutes won't make a massive difference. Another hour and three more episodes later, you check the time—it's almost 2 a.m. You feel ashamed and guilty because you know you've got work tomorrow, and now you won't get enough sleep. The next day you'll wake up exhausted and might have a headache all day which can only be cured by coffee. Then again, too much coffee will make you nauseous and anxious, which is not good for your health. If only you'd made the choice of going to bed after scrolling Instagram for 10 minutes as you planned.

The choices you make can impact your life in many different ways. Making good choices isn't something that most of us have been consciously taught, but we figured it out through trial and error. For instance, staying up till 2 a.m. on a work (or school) night is not a good choice because it can wreck the next day's schedule. The consequences of your choices can be heavy on your financial journey, too, which is why it is important to evaluate them and be careful. In this final chapter, we will be talking about how you can make rich choices and increase the efficiency of your decision-making process by overcoming fear and staying true to your intentions.

Rich and Poor Choices

Suppose you have a terrible cold and fever, but you still do not skip your daily iced coffee. Naturally, your cold will become even worse, and now it'll take you longer to recover. This is obviously a very bad choice, given the circumstances, and you shouldn't have drunk the iced coffee. For most things in life, there's no way to know whether a certain choice you made is good or bad unless it immediately affects you, like the event mentioned here. Your financial plans and decisions are slightly more complicated, which is why you need to be a bit more mindful of the choices you're making. In this section, we will be talking about rich and poor choices and how they affect your financial journey.

Examples of Poor Choices

Even though everyone has a different life and varying situations, there are some common bad choices that can prove to be quite harmful when you're trying to achieve financial freedom. Here are a few instances:

- **Creating a budget but never following it properly.** This usually happens when people copy someone else's budget and try to implement it in their own life. Since the goals and priorities don't match, the budget loses its value.

- **Spending money out of boredom.** When people have nothing to do, they might choose to look for ways to entertain themselves, and one of the ways is to spend money on random things. Thanks to the internet, nobody will ever run out of weird things to buy, and this goes to a whole other level when people are bored.

- **Not communicating money matters with their partner.** Many people like to maintain a sense of formality with their partners and go for months without talking about money. When they do, it's either something really insignificant or a huge fight about all the financial mistakes being made. The situation escalates further when both parties start blaming each other for their financial habits.

- **Spending too much money on convenience.** Eating out too frequently, never making coffee at home, and going to fancy juice places are all examples of overspending on convenience items. Everyone likes to feel comfortable, but that does not mean it is always okay to unrealistically spend money on things that can easily be made at home.

Examples of Rich Choices

If you look at the above bad choices and reverse the situations, you'll get a whole list of rich financial choices. For instance, following a budget properly and being mindful of your spending habits are great examples of good choices that can help you maintain harmony in your financial goals. Apart from these, here are some other good choices that you can make:

- **Start taking steps to be more productive.** Financial planning and management aren't limited to how much money you're making and the expenses being incurred. It has a lot to do with your attitude and how productive you are in your daily life. Simple things like maintaining a calendar, planning your day ahead, and keeping a to-do list can help you become a more disciplined person, which will, in turn, assist you in following through with your financial plans.

- **Invest in yourself.** We've already talked about the importance of investing in traditional education, but that's not all. You have to keep learning and enhancing your skills so that you can stay relevant in the professional world. Having in-demand skills will make it easier for you to keep your job or get new gigs in case something doesn't work out.

- **Learn from your mistakes.** Even if you are making all the right choices, you can still make some mistakes. Instead of blaming yourself, if you can learn from them and make an action plan to do better next time, you'll be able to make real progress.

- **Embrace new experiences.** When you move out after living with your parents for so many years, life might seem strange and confusing. You'll encounter all kinds of new things, but if you're not open to embracing them, you won't be able to build a new and exciting life. Even if some of the experiences seem daunting, doing them is a good choice because it broadens your horizons.

- **Become an organized person.** This is probably something that your parents have been telling you since you were a child, but choosing to be clean and organized is one of the best decisions you can make. Clean surroundings can help you think better and declutter your mind, which is one of the prerequisites of rational decision-making. Organization skills play an important role in your financial journey and prioritizing between your long-term and short-term goals.

Setting Financial Priorities

Throughout the different chapters of this book, we've talked at length about financial goals and setting priorities that resonate with your values. Now let's bring your choices into the discussion.

If you have a set of financial priorities that you wish to achieve within a certain timeframe, then your choices need to resonate with them. You cannot expect to fulfill your goals if you're not being true to yourself and deviating from your plan every chance you get. You might need to make some difficult choices for the sake of the greater good. For instance, if you're saving up for a house, you might not be able to go on fancy vacations for a while. It can feel frustrating but remember that you made the choice of buying a house your priority, and unless you stick with it, you won't be able to achieve it. It will all be worth it once you close the deal, sign the papers, and finally move into your dream house.

Having said that, you might also need to change your choices if the circumstances demand so. Suppose during this journey, you have an accident and require urgent medical care that is not entirely covered by your insurance. Then you've got to prioritize and make the choice of using the funds for your treatment. It all depends on the situation and its individual requirements.

Giving Back

When we talk about making good financial choices, charity and giving back aren't things that are mentioned right away. In fact, charity doesn't find its way into most finance-related conversations because everyone is very busy taking care of themselves, and they have no time to think about others. Granted, life is hard, and you have to constantly hustle to make a mark and afford all the things that you're planning for. But giving something back and helping others can have a profound impact on your mental health and financial plans. According to a study conducted by some professors at Harvard Business School and the University of British Columbia (2008), people who regularly participate in charitable activities and spend money on others exhibited higher happiness levels.

Being in a better mental state will enable you to make good financial choices and protect your money comprehensively. Here's how you can include the act of giving in your financial planning process:

- If you've never volunteered before, there's a high chance you won't be too thrilled with the whole "giving" thing. It doesn't make you a bad person at all, but it's just how our minds work. Start by combining the charity work with something that will add value to your work. You can do a good deed and benefit from it too. It won't make you a terrible person, but you'll get into the habit of charity work.

- Gradually align your financial goals with helping others. For instance, if you are planning to take a test to pursue higher education and you need to refresh your basic math skills, consider becoming a volunteer teacher for underprivileged kids

- Make sure you are enjoying the process of doing volunteer work. It should not be something that you're forced to do just for the sake of it. When you're doing things that you truly enjoy, you can give your best shot and actually make a difference.

Financial success isn't about achieving your own dreams but also creating a suitable environment for others to achieve theirs. The most successful businesspeople in the world are also some of the biggest philanthropists. Growth doesn't need to be limited to only you and your family. You can include others along the way and help them become the best version of themselves.

Modifying and Adjusting Choices

Life is constantly moving forward, and no matter how difficult it is to accept, we have to understand that it will change a lot. As a young adult, you will create a budget that resonates with your needs at that age. But it is highly likely that those needs will quickly change and get replaced with others that match your current priorities. During your late teens or early 20s, you might have a lot of dreams that are mostly centered around you and what you want to do. Your budget will also contain a list of financial goals that support these dreams. For example, you might want to backpack across Europe or buy a new car, and your budget will make savings and investment allocations to accommodate these expenses.

But as you grow older, your personal and professional commitments will make you want to rethink your financial goals. Suppose you had kept money aside for the down payment of a new car, but in the meantime, you get a great job offer that requires you to relocate. This is not an opportunity that you can turn down, but the relocation will require you to spend some big bucks. Buying a car might not be a priority at the moment since your new company will provide you with accommodation close to the office. So, the obvious thing to do here is to use your car funds for the relocation.

If you decide to get married and have kids, your financial priorities will once again shift dramatically. You'll want to save for your kids' education, buy more insurance, or think about moving into a bigger house. The point I'm trying to make here is that as life progresses, your financial goals will change, and you need to update your budget and plans accordingly. Even though a budget is supposed to be followed rigorously, it shouldn't be set in stone. When your lifestyle changes, your budget needs to change, too, so that it can continue serving its purpose. The key to making rich financial choices is to have a solid action plan and clarity about your goals. Misdirected plans are the biggest reason why people deviate from their paths, and you need to be careful not to fall into that trap.

The weird thing about wrong choices is that most of us are completely aware while making one. The problem isn't always being able to identify when you're making a poor choice, but to prevent yourself from making it in the first place. By now, you already know the impact of poor choices on your finances and why you should be aiming to make productive decisions at all costs. I do admit that it is easier said than done, but you've got to start somewhere. The path toward achieving financial freedom certainly isn't easy, but consistent good choices can lessen your struggles to a great extent.

Beginning this journey early in your life can help you in creating good financial habits. There will be some mistakes along the way, and you will make wrong decisions, but you have to be patient with yourself. If you beat yourself up for every misstep, you won't have the motivation left to continue anymore. Remember to stick to your budget and make notes when you are deviating a lot from your estimates. As you grow older, your priorities will shift, and you might need to modify your financial goals too. That is perfectly fine! Don't be hard on yourself because managing your finances is supposed to be an enjoyable thing. Work hard to earn money, and then let your money work for you. Trust your gut and take care of yourself in every phase of life. Things will get hard at times, and you might get awfully busy, but don't mess up your food and sleeping schedules, and remember to stay hydrated. If you're not okay, your financial plans won't be either. When things get overwhelming, remember your goals and let your own efforts inspire you. You deserve it!

Conclusion

Instead of buying a Mercedes, you can buy a Toyota; and then use the extra money that you would have spent every month, for about five years, on the installment, fuel, and insurance to buy shares in the company that owns Mercedes…or the one that owns Rolls-Royce. —Mokokoma Mokhonoana

As a child, I always dreamt of learning to play the guitar, but somehow, I could never manage to do it. At first, my parents didn't have the time to take me to lessons, and then I didn't have time because I got busy with my education. After moving out, it completely slipped my mind for a while as I started to focus on my career. I'm not gonna say I *never* got the time in all these years, but it just became one of those things that I never did. From time to time, I'd express my regret but not do anything to fix it.

This is basically the story of most people who are unable to work on their financial plans. No matter how much you blame your situation, achieving financial freedom is largely a matter of choice. You might not have been born into generational wealth, but you sure have the capabilities to create it during your lifetime. It all starts with being accountable for your financial situation. If something hasn't gone your way, take responsibility for it. Own your mistakes and learn from them so that you can do better next time. Acing financial planning isn't easy, which is why you have to remember the basics to protect your money at all costs.

It all starts with making that first budget and then keeping a close eye on it to see how you're doing. I'm not gonna lie, the budget is the foundation of the whole process, and it is crucial that you pay a lot of attention to it. It will also help you get more comfortable around money because you'll be neck-deep in making estimates and ensuring that you're following them. A budget is also the key to evaluating and eventually eliminating debt since it helps you become aware of how much you owe and how quickly you can repay all of it. Financial management becomes much easier when you have the basics covered, and you're taking active steps to protect your future. Start investing as early as you can. When you're young, you get plenty of time to earn good returns and even recover from any mishaps. Compounding helps you increase your money phenomenally over time, and by the time you're ready to retire, you'll find you've already saved up a fortune.

Your financial journey is unique, and you shouldn't compare it with others. I know when you open social media and everyone seems to be having the time of their lives, it can feel very frustrating. But trust me, comparison isn't going to get you anywhere. Stay true to your goals and share your journey only with the people closest to you. If you're living with your parents, you can think about talking to them. They might have some valuable insights to share and assist you in devising suitable strategies. If you're living with your partner, you should definitely discuss all money matters with them. There's no point in hiding your financial situation or how you feel about money because it will only lead to confusion and wrong decisions. If your partner doesn't seem interested in discussing money or if they make you feel uncomfortable about your situation, you might want to re-evaluate your relationship. I know it's hard to think of, but your partner needs to be your literal partner in everything, especially finances. Discussing money matters and creating a plan together is one of the best things you can do as a couple. Healthy relationships help foster a positive money mindset and allow you to achieve your financial goals faster.

Do you know what the scariest thing in the journey toward becoming a money master is? That it's all on you. The decisions you make, the steps you take, and the path you follow will lead you to your destination. But interestingly, that is also the best part of this journey. You get to do what you want to do. That kind of freedom is power. It motivates you to do better and be better because even though the climb is tough, the view from up there is worth it.

I know you'll do a good job with your finances because you decided to read this book all the way to the end. You're a rockstar, and you know it! You have learned all the necessary skills to become a money master, and now it's time to go out there and apply it. The beginning might be tough, but you've got to keep going because consistency is essential in the financial management process. You can always refer back to this book if you get stuck in something, we've got you! Good luck!

If you liked reading this book and it added value to your life, please be a Good Samaritan and leave a review for us. It will mean the world to us and help another reader like you in their financial management journey. Thank you!

References

Adams, S. (2013, April 1). *7 ways that generosity can lead to success.* Forbes. https://www.forbes.com/sites/susanadams/2013/04/01/7-ways-that-generosity-can-lead-to-success/?sh=7a6758b710c5

Alford, C. (2013, April 9). *50 money quotes by famous people that can change your attitude towards money.* Lifehack. https://www.lifehack.org/articles/money/50-money-quotes-by-famous-people-that-can-change-your-attitude-towards-money.html

Alison. (2023, July 13). *8 tips for making a budget when in your 20s.* Allwomenstalk. https://money.allwomenstalk.com/tips-for-making-a-budget-when-in-your-20s/

Banton, C. (2023, March 28). *Interest rates: Different types and what they mean to borrowers.* Investopedia. https://www.investopedia.com/terms/i/interestrate.asp#toc-apr-vs-apy

Benefits of investing. (2022, July 26). UK Capital and Income Investment Trust. https://www.columbiathreadneedle.co.uk/uk-capital-and-income-investment-trust-plc/insights/benefits-of-investing/

Bennett, K. (2023, January 17). *8 best money saving apps of 2023.* Bankrate. https://www.bankrate.com/banking/savings/best-money-saving-apps/#acorns

Bennett, R. (2022, October 4). *Short and long term financial goals: Top savings strategies for each.* Bankrate. https://www.bankrate.com/banking/savings/strategies-for-short-and-long-term-financial-goals/#what-are-goals

Brown, K. (2022, July 21). *7 steps for transforming your relationship with money.* Clever Girl Finance. https://www.clevergirlfinance.com/transforming-your-relationship-with-money/

Burton, N. (2014, April 2). *12 negative thoughts about money that are holding you back.* Business Insider. https://www.businessinsider.com/12-negative-thoughts-about-money-2014-4?op=1&r=US&IR=T

Cain, S. (2022, August 11). *10 common financial mistakes.* Prosper. https://www.prosper.com/blog/10-common-financial-mistakes

Caldwell, M. (2021, November 14). *Tips for preparing for unexpected financial events.* The Balance. https://www.thebalancemoney.com/planning-for-financial-emergencies-2385813

CFI Team. (2020, June 16). *Net worth.* Corporate Finance Institute. https://corporatefinanceinstitute.com/resources/valuation/net-worth/

CFI Team. (2022, November 28). *Financial literacy*. Corporate Finance Institute. https://corporatefinanceinstitute.com/resources/mana gement/financial-literacy/

Chen, J. (2023, February 28). *Debt: What it is, how it works, types, and ways to pay back*. Investopedia. https://www.investopedia.com/terms/d/debt.asp#toc -types-of-consumer-debt

Cheng, M. (2018, November 19). *These 9 bad habits and traits will keep you from your financial goals*. CNBC. https://www.cnbc.com/2018/11/19/these-9-bad-habits-and-traits-will-keep-you-from-your-financial-goals.html

Cox, K. (2012, April 17). *The 4 financial mistakes to avoid in your 20s*. The Muse. https://www.themuse.com/advice/the-4-financial-mistakes-to-avoid-in-your-20s

Cruze, R. (2022a, April 25). *How to set financial goals*. Ramsey Solutions. https://www.ramseysolutions.com/personal-growth/setting-financial-goals

Cruze, R. (2022b, November 8). *How to budget with a low income*. Ramsey Solutions. https://www.ramseysolutions.com/budgeting/how-to-budget-money-with-low-income

Cruze, R. (2023a, May 24). *How to change your money mindset*. Ramsey Solutions. https://www.ramseysolutions.com/budgeting/understa nding-your-money-mindset

Cruze, R. (2023b, May 24). *Understanding the psychology of money and what it's costing you*. Ramsey Solutions.

https://www.ramseysolutions.com/budgeting/psychol ogy-of-money

Dantus, C.-R. (2019, June 5). *Budgeting: How to create a budget and stick with it.* Consumer Financial Protection Bureau. https://www.consumerfinance.gov/about-us/blog/budgeting-how-to-create-a-budget-and-stick-with-it/

Dehan, A. (2021, September 23). *Rocket money.* Rocket Money. https://www.rocketmoney.com/learn/debt-and-credit/types-of-debt

DeMarco, J. (2020, January 9). *40% of people are making this crucial financial mistake—Are you one of them?* The Everygirl. https://theeverygirl.com/money-peer-pressure/

Depietro, A., & Lapera, G. (2022, August 25). *Average American debt by age and generation: 2022.* Credit Karma. https://www.creditkarma.com/insights/i/average-debt-by-age#average-total-debt-by-age-and-generation

Egan, J. (2021, July 30). *The debt avalanche method: How it works and how to use it.* Forbes Advisor. https://www.forbes.com/advisor/debt-relief/debt-avalanche-method-how-it-works/

Eneriz, A. (2023, May 16). *Debt avalanche vs. debt snowball: What's the difference?* Investopedia. https://www.investopedia.com/articles/personal-finance/080716/debt-avalanche-vs-debt-snowball-which-best-you.asp#toc-debt-avalanche-pros-and-cons

Estavillo, PsyD, D. M. (2020, July 15). *9 signs of a dysfunctional family.* Biltmore Psychology and Counseling.

https://www.biltmorecounseling.com/family/signs-of-a-dysfunctional-family/

15 life skills to master in your 20s. (n.d.). Skills You Need. https://www.skillsyouneed.com/rhubarb/life-skills-20s.html

Financial literacy quotes (20 quotes). (n.d.). Goodreads. https://www.goodreads.com/quotes/tag/financial-literacy

Financial tips: Six steps to creating a positive money mindset. (n.d.). Happy State Bank. https://www.happybank.com/resources/six-steps-to-creating-a-positive-money-mindset#:~:text=Work%20on%20Forming%20Good%20Habits

Five basic financial tips for young couples. (n.d.). SD Associates, P.C. https://www.sdaccounting.com/blog/five-basic-financial-tips-young-couples/

Fontinelle, A. (2019). *Start saving now! Here's why.* Investopedia. https://www.investopedia.com/articles/personal-finance/031215/why-saving-money-important.asp

Fries, T. (2023, January 17). *Millennial income statistics (2022): 100+ financial stats.* Tokenist. https://tokenist.com/millennial-income-statistics/#:~:text=Average%20Millennial%20Salary%20%F0%9F%93%8A

Furniss, M. (2016, March 14). *Common causes of debt.* Norton Finance. https://www.nortonfinance.co.uk/know-how/debt-management/common-causes-of-debt

Gillis, K. (2022, November 2). *10 unspoken rules of dysfunctional families.* Psychology Today. https://www.psychologytoday.com/us/blog/invisible-bruises/202211/10-unspoken-rules-dysfunctional-families

Gonzalez-Ribeiro, A. (2022, March 16). *50 empowering quotes on finances to help your money habits.* Self. https://www.self.inc/blog/quotes-on-finances

Gravier, E. (2021, January 7). *These top budgeting apps sync with your bank accounts, are widely available and come highly rated.* CNBC. https://www.cnbc.com/select/best-budgeting-apps/

Gregoire, C. (2018, February 8). *How money changes the way you think and feel.* Greater Good. https://greatergood.berkeley.edu/article/item/how_money_changes_the_way_you_think_and_feel

Hayes, A. (2021, August 20). *Investment.* Investopedia. https://www.investopedia.com/terms/i/investment.asp

Haynes, D. (2021, November 30). *How to negotiate with your creditors and settle your debts.* The Balance. https://www.thebalancemoney.com/how-to-negotiate-with-your-creditors-316120

Hitchcock-Gear, S. (2021, April 9). *The top 10 financial mistakes for young couples to avoid.* Kiplinger.com. https://www.kiplinger.com/personal-finance/602575/the-top-10-financial-mistakes-for-young-couples-to-avoid

Honda, K. (2021a). *Self-made millionaire: This is the easiest way to start investing for retirement.* CNBC. https://www.cnbc.com/2021/04/28/7-money-personality-types-and-the-pitfalls-of-each.html

Honda, K. (2021b). *There are 7 money personality types, says psychology expert. Which one are you?* CNBC. https://www.cnbc.com/2021/04/28/7-money-personality-types-and-the-pitfalls-of-each.html

How to overcome 8 kinds of financial problems & difficulties. (2018, December 11). My Money Coach. https://www.mymoneycoach.ca/blog/how-to-overcome-financial-problems-difficulties

Hughes, K. (2018, October 4). *25 of the best planning quotes.* ProjectManager. https://www.projectmanager.com/blog/planning-quotes

Ifeoma Olisakwe, P. (2023, January 25). *6 proven ways to maintain a debt-free lifestyle.* Preciousifeoma.com. https://preciousifeoma.com/6-proven-ways-to-maintain-a-debt-free-lifestyle/

The importance of financial literacy. (2019, April 29). Business Review at Berkeley. https://businessreview.berkeley.edu/the-importance-of-financial-literacy/

Irby, L. (2021a, November 27). *What's the difference between good debt and bad debt?* The Balance. https://www.thebalancemoney.com/good-debt-vs-bad-debt-960029

Irby, L. (2021b, December 28). *5 ways to reduce your monthly debt payments.* The Balance. https://www.thebalancemoney.com/ways-to-lower-debt-payments-960853

Jabs, M. (2010, January 21). *Celebrate debt reduction milestones.* Dough Roller. https://fivecentnickel.com/celebrate-debt-reduction-milestones-dfa/

James, M. (2016, April 6). *8 beliefs you should have about money.* Psychology Today. https://www.psychologytoday.com/us/blog/focus-forgiveness/201604/8-beliefs-you-should-have-about-money

Jespersen, C. (2020, May 13). *How to save money: 17 tips.* NerdWallet. https://www.nerdwallet.com/article/finance/how-to-save-money

Kaufman, R. (2017, April 26). *Financial attitude and financial literacy.* My FICO. https://www.myfico.com/credit-education/blog/financial-attitude-and-financial-literacy

Lazar, A. (2021, June 21). *Money scripts: Understanding your relationship with money.* FinMasters. https://finmasters.com/money-scripts/

Marelisa. (2013, June 12). *35 powerful beliefs about money: From Trump to the Dalai Lama.* Daring to Live Fully. https://daringtolivefully.com/powerful-beliefs-about-money

Marter, J. (2021, August 28). *How your parents' beliefs about money affect you.* Psychology Today https://www.psychologytoday.com/gb/blog/mental-wealth/202108/how-your-parents-beliefs-about-money-affect-you

Martin, E. (2020, December 22). *How to align your personal values with your financial goals.* Linked in. https://www.linkedin.com/pulse/how-align-your-personal-values-financial-goals-ember-martin-cfp/

McConnell, A. (2018, September 5). *Council post: Why continuous education matters.* Forbes. https://www.forbes.com/sites/theyec/2018/09/05/why-continuous-education-matters/?sh=72970746320f

Morris, C. (2021, February 26). *Understanding the main types of debt and how to pay them off.* Money Geek. https://www.moneygeek.com/debt/

Murphy, C. B. (2022). *Understanding the cash flow statement.* Investopedia. https://www.investopedia.com/investing/what-is-a-cash-flow-statement/

Nannini, A. (2022, August 15). *7 ways to maintain a consumer debt free lifestyle.* Cash Uncomplicated. https://cashuncomplicated.com/7-ways-to-maintain-a-consumer-debt-free-lifestyle/

Norris, E. (2022, June 14). *Top 10 most common financial mistakes.* Investopedia. https://www.investopedia.com/personal-finance/most-common-financial-mistakes/

O'Shea, B., & Pyles□, S. (2023, February 22). *How to use the debt snowball method to pay off debt.* NerdWallet. https://www.nerdwallet.com/article/finance/what-is-a-debt-snowball

O'Shea, B., & Schwahn, L. (2021, January 13). *Budgeting 101: How to budget money.* NerdWallet. https://www.nerdwallet.com/article/finance/how-to-budget

Owens, E. (2021, December 9). *Wealth mindset - 6 ways to develop it in your mind.* Antimaximalist. https://antimaximalist.com/wealth-mindset/

Pyles, S. (2021, August 6). *Debt settlement negotiations: A do-it-yourself guide.* NerdWallet. https://www.nerdwallet.com/article/finance/debt-settlement-negotiations

Pyles, S. (2023, February 21). *Good debt vs. bad debt: Examples and solutions.* NerdWallet. https://www.nerdwallet.com/article/finance/good-debt-vs-bad-debt

Ramsey Solutions. (2022, August 23). *10 characteristics of debt-free living.* Ramsey Solutions. https://www.ramseysolutions.com/debt/7-characteristics-of-debt-free-people

Ramsey Solutions. (2023, May 8). *Car depreciation: How much is your car worth?* Ramsey Solutions. https://www.ramseysolutions.com/saving/car-depreciation#:~:text=After%20one%20year%2C%20your%20car

Raypole, C. (2021, January 20). *Positive peer pressure: Examples, effects, and more.* Healthline. https://www.healthline.com/health/positive-peer-pressure

Regain Editorial Team. (2019). *How to recognize when you're in a dysfunctional relationship—And what to do if you are.* Regain. https://www.regain.us/advice/general/how-to-recognize-when-youre-in-a-dysfunctional-relationship-and-what-to-do-if-you-are/

Relationships quotes (11230 quotes). (n.d.). Goodreads. https://www.goodreads.com/quotes/tag/relationships

Robinson, L. (2018, November 2). *Tips for building a healthy relationship.* Help Guide. https://www.helpguide.org/articles/relationships-communication/relationship-help.htm

Romanelli, A. (2019, August 8). *Let's talk about money in our intimate relationships!* Psychology Today. https://www.psychologytoday.com/us/blog/the-other-side-relationships/201908/lets-talk-about-money-in-our-intimate-relationships

Rose, S. (2022, September 14). *The 12 biggest financial mistakes to avoid in your 20s.* OppLoans. https://www.opploans.com/oppu/articles/financial-mistakes-to-avoid-in-your-20s/

SBO Editorial Team. (2023, May 3). *What is a balance sheet: Understanding the basics of financial statements.* SBO. https://sbo.sg/business/management/what-is-balance-sheet/

Schwahn, L. (2022, December 5). *Free budget planner worksheet.* NerdWallet. https://www.nerdwallet.com/article/finance/budget-worksheet

Scott, S. (2019, February 22). *How to invest in yourself: 33 ways to change your life's potential.* Happier Human. https://www.happierhuman.com/invest-in-yourself/

Seven ways your dysfunctional relationship is making you poor. (2015). Nasdaq.com. https://www.nasdaq.com/articles/7-ways-your-dysfunctional-relationship-making-you-poor-2015-10-22

Silva Casabianca , S. (2021, May 6). *15 cognitive distortions to blame for your negative thinking.* Psych Central. https://psychcentral.com/lib/cognitive-distortions-negative-thinking#list-and-examples

Snider, S. (2019). *How to handle relationships and money.* US News & World Report; U.S. News & World Report. https://money.usnews.com/money/personal-finance/family-finance/articles/how-to-handle-relationships-and-money

Sokunbi, B. (2022, March 6). *11 key ways to improve your money mindset.* Clever Girl Finance. https://www.clevergirlfinance.com/how-you-can-improve-your-money-mindset/

Success, F. (2020, November 13). *How to develop a positive money mindset.* Brian Tracy's Self Improvement & Professional Development Blog. https://www.briantracy.com/blog/financial-success/how-to-develop-a-positive-money-mindset/

The Finance Therapist. (2021, December 17). *13 financial thought patterns holding you back.* The Finance Therapist. https://thefinancetherapist.com/13-financial-thought-patterns-holding-you-back/

Thirteen examples of good and bad spending habits. (2021, December 10). PenFed Credit Union. https://www.penfed.org/learn/good-and-bad-spending-habits

Top 25 freedom of choice quotes (of 125). (n.d.). A-Z Quotes. https://www.azquotes.com/quotes/topics/freedom-of-choice.html

Treleaven, S. (2018, June 26). *The science behind happy relationships.* Time. https://time.com/5321262/science-behind-happy-healthy-relationships/

Understanding your money beliefs: Knowledge is power. (n.d.). Aspen Wealth Management. https://www.aspenwealthmgmt.com/resource-center/blog/understanding-money-beliefs

Unhealthy money attitudes (and how to change yours). (2017, September 11). Penny Pinchin Mom. https://pennypinchinmom.com/identify-money-attitude/

Walsh, C. (2008, April 17). *Money spent on others can buy happiness.* Harvard Gazette. https://news.harvard.edu/gazette/story/2008/04/money-spent-on-others-can-buy-happiness/

Ward, R. (2019, January 9). *Benefit mindset 101: A simple explanation for a simply beautiful concept.* Robert Ward's "Rewarding Education" Blog for Teachers and Parents. https://rewardingeducation.wordpress.com/2019/01/09/benefit-mindset-101-a-simple-explanation-for-a-simply-beautiful-concept/

Wealth, A.-L. (2022, March 17). *How to build wealth when you don't come from money.* Harvard Business Review. https://hbr.org/2022/03/how-to-build-wealth-when-you-dont-come-from-money

What are the different types of consumer debt? (n.d.). Equifax. https://www.equifax.com/personal/education/debt-management/types-of-consumer-debts/

What is a wealth mindset? (n.d.). Build Wealth 4 Real People. https://www.buildwealth4realpeople.com/blog/what-is-a-wealth-mindset

Why investing is important | Wells Fargo Advisors. (n.d.). Wells Fargo. https://www.wellsfargo.com/goals-investing/why-invest/#:~:text=Why%20is%20investing%20important%3F

Woodard, D. (2022, September 15). *Basic budgeting tips everyone should know.* The Balance. https://www.thebalancemoney.com/budgeting-101-1289589

Made in the USA
Las Vegas, NV
21 December 2023

83328681R00079